BIRDS, BEASTS, AND SEAS

NATURE POEMS FROM NEW DIRECTIONS

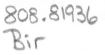

BIRDS, BEASTS, AND SEAS

NATURE POEMS FROM NEW DIRECTIONS

EDITED BY JEFFREY YANG

A New Directions Book

Manufactured in the United States of America
New Directions Books are printed on acid-free paper
First published as a New Directions Paperbook Original (NDP1196) in 2011
Published simultaneously in Canada by Penguin Books Canada Limited

Library of Congress Cataloging-in-Publication Data
(Birds, Beasts, and Seas: Nature Poems from New Directions / edited by Jeffrey Yang.—1st American Pbk. ed.
    p. cm.
  "A New Directions Book."
Includes bibliographical references and index.
    ISBN 978-0-8112-1919-8 (pbk.: alk. paper)
    1. Nature—Poetry. I. Yang, Jeffrey. II. New Directions Publishing Corp.
PS595.N22.B57 2011
808.81'936—dc22
                  2010040874

10 9 8 7 6 5 4 3 2

New Directions Books are published for James Laughlin
by New Directions Publishing Corporation
80 Eighth Avenue, New York, NY 10011

"Will I ever reach the aim that I've so long pursued and searched for?

"I am still working from nature and feel I am making a little progress."

—Paul Cezanne, September 1906,
a few weeks before his death

…duce ac magistra natura

CONTENTS

PREFACE

What is nature? Physis, growth. Its root means "to be born." Spinoza, for one, equated the world with God and God with nature. Goethe saw his own poetry as "simply nature" and nature itself as a "spiritual emanation in which we could discover the secrets of our own life." Emerson also experienced nature as spirit, "a perpetual effect" that "puts it forth through us, as the life of the tree puts forth new branches and leaves through the pores of the old." When Emerson inquires, "To what end is nature?," nature is understood as, on the one hand, "the essences unchanged by man" (i.e. sky, river, leaf) and on the other hand, to the classical Western philosopher, all that is not the Soul, or "a metaphor of the human mind" for, according to Plotinus, the Soul is wisdom and nature doesn't know. A century after Emerson, the poet Paul Valéry observes, "Whenever we run across something we do not know how to make but that appears to be made, we say that nature produced it." Japanese philosopher Kojin Karatani extends Valéry's thought in our times when he writes, "Nature, therefore, is not restricted to ostensibly natural objects such as the seashell; it also includes things that are made by man but whose structure—how they are made—is not immediately discernible. Such things are called natural language because their making is not apparent." Nature here is provisional, and inseparable from our own thinking and perceptions—it circumscribes the limits of our own making as what nature makes is a part of what humans make. Who was the wise child who said, "Nature makes my teeth 'to hurt'"?

In the land and days of Mencius (China, 4th century B.C.), nature 性 (*xing*) usually referred to "human nature." It is interesting to note that the character 性 itself is composed of two other words: the left radical 心 (*xin*) meaning "heart, mind, or moral nature"; and the right side 生 (*sheng*) meaning "to give birth to." This combination of pictographs certainly infuses Mencius's thought: the heart-mind giving birth to moral nature that in turn shapes human nature. A generation after Mencius, Xunzi composed his 天 論 (*Tian lun*), often translated into English as "Discussion of Heaven" or "Discussion of Nature." The work opens with the line: "As *Tian* maintains the constant course of the heavenly bodies [morality], it acted in no special way toward Yao's survival or toward Jie's fall." (Yao and Jie are ancient kings.) This line is cited in a standard Chinese dictionary for classical Chinese under the second definition for the character *Tian* (天)signifying the natural world, 自 然 (*zi ran*). Today自 然 is the common Chinese phrase used for nature as referring to Emerson's "essences unchanged by man," and literally means "self-rightness." How an estimated ninety percent of China's groundwater came to be contaminated in the industrial age shows how far removed we've grown from language. Nature is as transmutable as heaven. Or take this description by Sartre of Baudelaire: "His ambition was the solitude which belongs to the accursed and the monster, to 'counter-nature' precisely because Nature is everything and everywhere."

Considering the nature poem, Frank O'Hara's comment about nature in painting thus seems to speak for nature in poetry: it depends on the historical period. Nature, being multivalent and as fluid as our identities or a river, reflects the changing times. It may be as eternally indifferent as the sun beating down on the rich and poor alike, but it is very much involved in the miracle of understanding, the "infectious—ecstasy" of H.D's biological reality. And as far back as words have existed poets have pursued this miracle by composing poems of, about, for, to, in and around, nature. Poets have asked and nature has answered, often with more questions, heavenly or otherwise. If nature loves to hide, as Herakleitos says, then poetry has been lured into its most secret places of becoming.

2011 marks the seventy-fifth anniversary of New Directions Publishing. The press began as a publisher of international avant-garde literature, and continues today—small and independent—in the spirit of its founder, James Laughlin, by publishing exciting, innovative literary works from the U.S. and around the world. If the term "avant-garde" felt outdated twenty-five years ago, it is worth remembering that this word once described a recognizable range of writers and artists who were actively resisting the suffocating cultural, socio-political calcifications of their day—a word, George Oppen wrote, "understood as referring not to exiled groups, but to the heart of the matter." They were aware that good poetry, like nature, requires constant renewal and regeneration through time. This is the publishing vision that still guides New Directions in bringing the books of living authors, and the forgotten classics of departed masters, to forgiving English readers.

Birds, Beasts, and Seas draws from the whole of ND's long-tailed library. A handful of poems were pulled from anthologies, most from individual poetry collections, a few from plays, one from a novel, and one from Gustav Janouch's *Conversations with Kafka*. ND has over a thousand titles in print and the bulk of the poems in this book can be traced to an in-print volume. Those titles now out of print were either originally published as a limited edition, or at the time too costly to reprint, or the rights reverted back to the author, another publisher, or literary estate. Structurally, the collection is arranged chronologically by each poet's birth-year, opening with a few ancient poems of China, Greece, Rome, Japan, India, and Persia, then dipping briefly into the Troubadour, Renaissance, and Elizabethan periods before blossoming into a constellation of poets from the nineteenth and twentieth centuries, crossing movements and schools, geographies and cultures, into our present. Usually only one poem or a section of one poem by each poet has been selected in order to present the widest range of ND poets within the limits of this edition. But this limitation has its benefits, too, as poets rub directly against their peers, poem to poem, while connecting threads between poems are heightened and lines from distant times and places converse with one another—all in the splendors and shadows of nature. Choices were made in the spirit of this conversation so that the book can be considered as a linked whole. This crisscrossing of cultures and ages, the constant translation of the present through the past, is fertile soil for poetry. That translation reinvigorates language and culture, and has been a pivotal practice for American poets from the last century into this one, is evident in these pages. One also gets a bird's eye view of how nature in poetry has evolved and subsisted over the centuries as each generation of poets is reborn into the next. These, at least, are a few of the hopes and pleasures of this celebratory little anthology, which, to echo a geologic phrase from the title of Forrest Gander's new book, gives a subjective, natural *core sample* of not only the history of New Directions, but of modern and contemporary international poetry. A different sample within these constraints would shift the light and lacunae though the nature of the record would remain unchanged.

"To use words rarely is to be natural," Lao Zi says. Hidden within the following pages the reader may discover some of the rarest words arranged in their most natural order ever to appear in English. It is a rareness that poetry, like any art, offers us—a common, transcendent value that is based on a shared experience. Over the centuries, the human beast has consistently trampled the planet's nature out of nature so that today, the scale of the destruction of nature has become a moral imperative of the most critical order. All the chlorinated hydrocarbons derived from petroleum and salts are man-made and otherwise never found in earth's mantle-lithosphere: the solvents, plastics, pesticides, and transportation-industry wastes filling air, land, and sea have real but immeasurable consequences. In this present of our own making and unmaking, perhaps a nature poem could, on one level, help focus our attention into an awareness of thought and need—as deeds follow the heels of words, each uniting the other. Robert Duncan translates Gérard de Nerval:

> Respect in the animal an active intellect:
> Each flower is a soul in Nature bloomd forth;
> A mystery of love lies conceald in the metal;
>   "Everything is sentient!"

Can any poem be called a nature poem after it is written, the way any event can be called history after the event's passed? Is it then a question of degree and context? To paraphrase Karatani, nature is the negative figure at the heart of our making. Nature is complexity in simplicity. Nature is a god in ruins. Nature is a rightness of self. Nature is constant regeneration.
Nature lets us speak. (Poetry is its excess.)

—*Jeffrey Yang*
Spring 2011

BIRDS, BEASTS, AND SEAS

NATURE POEMS FROM NEW DIRECTIONS

ANONYMOUS (c. 1000 B.C.)

From *The Book of Odes*

Heaven conserve thy course in quietness,
Solid thy unity, thy weal endless
that all the crops increase and nothing lack
in any common house.

Heaven susteyne thy course in quietness
that thou be just in all, and reap
so, as it were at ease, that every day
seem festival.

Heaven susteyne thy course in quietness
To abound and rise as mountain hill and range
constant as rivers flow that all augment
steady th' increase in ever cyclic change.

Pure be the victuals of thy sacrifice
throughout the year as autumns move to springs,
above the fane to hear "ten thousand years"
spoke by the manes of foregone dukes and kings.

Spirits of air assign felicity:
thy folk be honest, in food and drink delight;
dark-haired the hundred tribes concord
in act born of thy true insight.

As moon constant in phase; as sun to rise;
as the south-hills nor crumble nor decline;
as pine and cypress evergreen the year
be thy continuing line.

Translated from the Chinese by Ezra Pound

SAPPHO (7th century B.C.)

"Come out of Crete"

Come out of Crete
And find me here,
Come to your grove,
Mellow apple trees
And holy altar
Where the sweet smoke
Of libanum is in
Your praise,

Where leaf melody
In the apples
Is a crystal crash,
And the water is cold.
All roses and shadow,
This place, and sleep
Like dusk sifts down
From trembling leaves.

Here horses stand
In flowers and graze.
The wind is glad
And sweet in its moving
Here, Kypris [   ].
Pour nectar in the golden cups
And mix it deftly with
Our dancing and mortal wine.

Translated from the Greek by Guy Davenport

HERAKLEITOS (5th century B.C.)

"The Logos is eternal"

The Logos is eternal
but men have not heard it
and men have heard it and not understood.

Through the Logos all things are understood
yet men do not understand
as you shall see when you put acts and words to the test
I am going to propose:

One must talk about everything according to its nature,
how it comes to be and how it grows.
Men have talked about the world without paying attention
to the world or to their own minds,
as if they were asleep or absent-minded.

Translated from the Greek by Guy Davenport

EURIPIDES (480–406 B.C.)

From *Hippolytus Temporizes*

Phaedra   O grace of wild, wild things,
                     O swallow fair,
                     O fair sea-swallow,
                     flitting here and there,
                     O swallow,
                     beating with insatiate wing,
                     the very pulse and centre of the air,
                     O swallow, swallow,
                     listening everywhere—

Myrrhina   What is this fever,
                     this impassioned prayer?

Phaedra   —you took,
                     you severed with blue wing and fire,
                     the very salt wind,
                     to deliver there,
                     back in bright Crete,
                     my message and my prayer.

Myrrhina   Whom do you call,
                     O mistress,
                     by this shrine?

Phaedra   I cry,
                     I call again
                     to her
                     who makes the birds her message-bearer
                     to her
                     who yokes the swallows to her car.

Translated from the Greek by H.D.

From *Medea*

First Woman   The holy fountains flow up from the earth,
                 The smoke of sacrifice flows up from
                      the earth,
                 The eagle and the wild swan fly up from
                      the earth,
                 Righteousness also
                 Has flown up from the earth to the
                      feet of God.
                 It is not here, but up there; peace and
                      pity are departed;
                 Hatred is here; hatred is heavy, it clings to
                      the earth.
                 Love blows away, hatred remains.

                         . . .

Second Woman   Blood is the seed of blood, hundredfold
                      the harvest,
                 The gleaners that follow it, their feet
                      are crimson—

First Woman   I see the whirlwind hanging from the
                      black sky
                 Like a twisted rope,
                 Like an erect serpent, its tail tears the earth,
                 It is braided of dust and lightning,
                 Who will fly in it? Let me hide myself
                 From these night-shoring pillars and the
                      dark door.

Translated from the Greek by Robinson Jeffers

PRINCE ILANGÔ ADIGAL (3rd century B.C.)

From **The Blessings**
Mangalavâlttuppâdal

Blessed be the Moon!
Blessed be the Moon that wraps the Earth
in misty veils of cooling light,
and looms, a royal parasol
festooned with pollen-laden flowers,
protecting us.

Blessed be the Sun!
Blessed be the Sun that, endless pilgrim,
slowly circles round the axial mountain,
image of the royal emblem
of the beloved monarch of the land
where the Kâverî flows.

Blessed be the mighty clouds!
Blessed be the mighty clouds that on the Earth
shower down rain as generous
as he who rules the land
a raging sea surrounds.

Blessed be Puhâr, city of wonders!
Blessed be the city of wonders,
immortal testimony to the power
of a glorious line of kings
whose fame has spread to every land
the boundless sea surrounds.

Translated from the Tamil by Alain Daniélou

MELEAGROS (1st century B.C.)

Flowers: For Hêliodôra.

White violets I'll bring
And soft narcissus
And myrtle and laughing lilies
The innocent crocus
Dark hyacinth also
And roses heavy with love

And these I'll twine for Hêliodôra
And scatter the bright petals on her hair

Translated from the Greek by Dudley Fitts

LUCRETIUS (99–55 B.C.)

"Darling of Gods and Men"

Darling of Gods and Men, beneath the gliding stars
you fill rich earth and buoyant sea with your presence
for every living thing achieves its life through you,
rises and sees the sun. For you the sky is clear,
the tempests still. Deft earth scatters her gentle flowers,
the level ocean laughs, the softened heavens glow
with generous light for you. In the first days of spring
when the untrammelled allrenewing southwind blows
the birds exult in you and herald your coming.
Then the shy cattle leap and swim the brooks for love.
Everywhere, through all seas mountains and waterfalls,
love caresses all hearts and kindles all creatures
to overmastering lust and ordained renewals.
Therefore, since you alone control the sum of things
and nothing without you comes forth into the light
and nothing beautiful or glorious can be
without you, Alma Venus! trim my poetry
with your grace; and give peace to write and read and think.

Translated from the Latin by Basil Bunting

VIRGIL (70–19 B.C.)

From *Georgics: I*

Until Jove let it be, no colonist
Mastered the wild earth; no land was marked,
None parceled out or shared; but everyone
Looked for his living in the common wold.

And Jove gave poison to the blacksnakes, and
Made the wolves ravage, made the ocean roll,
Knocked honey from the leaves, took fire away—
So man might beat out various inventions
By reasoning and art.
                              First he chipped fire
Out of the veins of flint where it was hidden;
Then rivers felt his skiffs of the light alder;
Then sailors counted up the stars and named them:
Pleiades, Hyades, and Pole Star;
Then were discovered ways to take wild things.
In snares, or hunt them with the circling pack;
And how to whip a stream with casting nets,
Or draw the deep-sea fisherman's cordage up;
And then the use of steel and the shrieking saw;
Then various crafts. All things were overcome
By labor and by force of bitter need.

Translated from the Latin by Robert Fitzgerald

KING SHUDRAKA (c. 1 B.C.–1 A.D.)

From *The Toy Cart*

Maitreya, to   The storm has started again, and the rain is
Charudatta   simply tumbling down.

Charudatta   How well you put it.
                       The rains pierce through the clouds, as
                            lotus roots
                       Pierce the soil, softly, as if
                       Weeping for the absent moon.
                       My dearest, look at the sky, black-haired,
                            scented with wind.
                       The lightning scoops her into his arms.
                       Tenderly but fiercely, as lover does lover.

Vasantasena, unable to control her feelings, embraces him.
Charudatta puts his arms around her.

                       Let the clouds alone, Maitreya.
                       Let it rain a hundred years,
                       A hundred years of thunder, a hundred
                            of lightning.
                       They are my friends:
                       They have given me my love.
                       My love is in my arms.
                       Happy is he who embraces his love
                            in the rain.
                       Vasantasena, dearest, the door creaks,
                       The walls are miserably wet;
                       The mortar is cracked, the roof will leak—
                       Nothing will last.
                       Oh, see the tongue of lightning licking
                            the yawning sky!

But now look, look at the rainbow!
See how its arms rise in holy prayer!
Now it is time to sleep.
Sleep will come sweeter with these
    pebbly drops
Splattering on palm leaves, falling on
    brooks;
Like a lute, and a voice singing,
Like a lute—the rain, and the music
    of the rain.

Translated from the Sanskrit by P. Lal

OVID (43 B.C.–18 A.D.)

From *Amores* [Book I, Elegy 13]

Now on the sea from her olde loue comes shee
That drawes the day from heaven's cold axle-tree,
Aurora whither slidest thou down againe,
And brydes from Memnon yeerly shall be slaine,

Now in her tender arms I sweetlie bide,
If euer, now well lies she by my side,
The ayre is colde, and sleep is sweetest now,
And byrdes send foorth shrill notes from every bow.
Whither runst thou, that men and women loue not?

Holde in thy rosie horses that they moue not!
Ere thou rise, stars teach seamen where to saile
But when thou comest, they of their courses faile.
Poore trauilers though tired rise at thy sight,
The painful Hinde by thee to fild is sent,
Slow oxen early in the yoke are pent,
Thou cousenest boys of sleep and dost betray them
To Pedants that with cruel lashes pay them.

Translated from the Latin by Christopher Marlowe

T'AO CH'IEN (364–427)

Turning Seasons

Turning seasons turning wildly
away, morning's majestic calm

unfolds. Out in spring clothes,
I roam eastern fields. Lingering

clouds sweep mountains clean.
Gossamer mist blurs open skies.

And soon, feeling south winds,
young grain ripples like wings.

Translated from the Chinese by David Hinton

From *Dwelling in the Mountain*

Abiding by spring and autumn
trusting morning and night,

we plow our own fields for food
and coax mulberries into cloth,

grow vegetables for tender treats
and gather herbs to ease old age.

Elsewhere no concern of mine
I follow my nature without doubts:

I listen to dharma in the morning
and set animals free at nightfall,

savor the inner pattern in books
and render my own mind in song.

Giving voice here to my thoughts,
I trust the steady play of details,

shape them into a weave of words
according to their impulse alone.

Translated from the Chinese by David Hinton

CH'U CH'UANG I (early 8th century)

A Mountain Spring

There is a brook in the mountains,
Nobody I ask knows its name.
It shines on the earth like a piece
Of the sky. It falls away
In waterfalls, with a sound
Like rain. It twists between rocks
And makes deep pools. It divides
Into islands. It flows through
Calm reaches. It goes its way
With no one to mind it. The years
Go by, its clear depths never change.

Translated from the Chinese by Kenneth Rexroth

YAMABE NO AKAHITO (700–736)

THREE POEMS

In Waka Bay when
The tide covers the sand bars
The cranes fly across
To the reeds of the other
Shore, making great cries.

*

On Fujiyama
Under the midsummer moon
The snow melts, and falls
Again the same night.

*

The mists rise over
The still pools at Asuka.
Memory does not
Pass away so easily.

Translated from the Japanese by Kenneth Rexroth

WANG WEI (701–761)

Climbing to Subtle-Aware Monastery

A bamboo path begins at the very beginning,
wanders up past Chimera City to lotus peaks

where windows look out across all of Ch'u
and nine rivers run smooth above forests.

Grasses cushion legs sitting *ch'an* stillness
up here. Towering pines echo pure chants.

Inhabiting emptiness beyond dharma cloud,
we see through human realms to unborn life.

Translated from the Chinese by David Hinton

LI PO (701–762)

**Night Thoughts at East-Forest Monastery
on Thatch-Hut Mountain**

Alone, searching for blue-lotus roofs,
I set out from city gates. Soon, frost

clear, East-Forest temple bells call out,
Tiger Creek's moon bright in pale water.

Heaven's fragrance everywhere pure
emptiness, heaven's music endless,

I sit silent. It's still, the entire Buddha-
realm in hair's-breadth, mind-depths

all bottomless clarity, in which vast
kalpas begin and end out of nowhere.

Translated from the Chinese by David Hinton

TU FU (712–770)

Written on the Wall at Chang's Hermitage

It is Spring in the mountains.
I come alone seeking you.
The sound of chopping wood echoes
Between the silent peaks.
The streams are still icy.
There is snow on the trail.
At sunset I reach your grove
In the stony mountain pass.
You want nothing, although at night
You can see the aura of gold
And silver ore around you.
You have learned to be gentle
As the mountain deer you have tamed.
They way back forgotten, hidden
Away, I become like you,
An empty boat, floating, adrift.

Translated from the Chinese by Kenneth Rexroth

Evening Rain

An early cricket sings clear, then stops.
A lamp flickers out, then flares up again.

Outside the window, telling me evening
rain's come: a clattering in banana trees.

Translated from the Chinese by David Hinton

MANUCHEHRI (982–1040)

"The thundercloud fills meadows"

The thundercloud fills meadows with heavenly beauty,
gardens with plants, embroiders plants with petals,
distils from its own white pearls brilliant dyes,
makes a Tibet of hills where its shadow falls,
San'a of our fields when it passes on to the desert.
Wail of the morning nightingale, scent of the breeze,
frenzy a man's bewildered, drunken heart.
Now is the season lovers shall pant awhile,
now is the day sets hermits athirst for wine.

Shall I sulk because my love has a double heart?
Happy is he whose she is singlehearted!
She has found me a new torment for every instant
and I am, whatever she does, content, content.
If she has bleached my cheek with her love, say: Bleach!
Is not pale saffron prized above poppy red?
If she has stooped my shoulders, say to them: Stoop!
Must not a harp be bent when they string it to sing?
If she has kindled fire in my heart, say: Kindle!
Only the kindled candle sends forth light.
If tears rain from my eyes, say: Let them rain!
Spring rains make fair gardens. And if then
she has cast me into the shadow of exile, say:
Those who seek fortune afar find it the first.

Translated from the Persian by Basil Bunting

GOLIARD POET (10–11th century)

A Summer Song of Birds

Delicate leafage decks the gloom of woodlands,
See how the boughs with fruit are heavy laden;
High in the tree-tops all the pigeons perching
      Murmur their carols.

Moaning of doves and thrushes' flutelike music
Blend with the blackbirds' never changing whistle;
Sparrows unquiet, high beneath the elm-tree,
      Laughingly chatter,

Glad in the branches nightingales are singing,
Hark! in the air the notes prolonged and stately
Vibrate; the kite is shaking down from heaven
      Tremulous outcries.

Up to the stars the eagle soars; the lark too
Rises in the air and frees his tuneful measures;
Sweet is his mounting song, he sings another
      Earthward descending.

Sounding his clamor, darts the rapid swallow,
Quail like to drum, while shrill the jackdaws twitter;
Everywhere singing, all the birds together
      Honor the summer.

Think of the bee, for not a bird is like him,
None is a type of chastity more perfect,
Only excelled by her whose spotless bosom
      Pillowed the Christ-child.

Translated from the Latin by George F. Whicher

LI CH'ING-CHAO (1084–1151)

Two Springs

Spring has come to the Pass.
Once more the new grass is kingfisher green.
The pink buds of the peach trees
Are still unopened little balls.
The clouds are milk white jade
Bordered and spotted with green jade.
No dust stirs.
In a dream that was too easy to read,
I have already drained and broken
The cup of Spring.
Flower shadows lie heavy
On the translucent curtains.
The full, transparent moon
Rises in the orange twilight.
Three times in two years
My lord has gone away to the East.
Today he returns.
And my joy is already
Greater than the Spring.

Translated from the Chinese by Kenneth Rexroth and Ling Chung

RASHIDI SAMARQANDI (c. 1100)

Complaint to a Court Poet

You say my poetry
lacks spice
not enough Freud
and too little vice.
You may be right.

My lines are soft and sweet as new-mown hay
just the place for nature's play.

I leave to you
the public's taste
for sorrel, vinegar
and human waste.

Translated from the Persian by Omar Pound

SA'DI (c. 1184–1283)

"Night swallowed the sun"

Night swallowed the sun as
the fish swallowed Jonas.

Translated from the Persian by Basil Bunting

ARNAUT DANIEL (12–13th century)

"When I see leaf, and flower and fruit"

When I see leaf, and flower and fruit
    Come forth upon light lynd and bough,
And hear the frogs in rillet bruit,
    And birds quhitter in forest now,
Love inkirlie doth leaf and flower and bear,
And trick my night from me, and stealing waste it,
Whilst other wight in rest and sleep sojourneth.

Translated from the Provençal by Ezra Pound

GEOFFREY CHAUCER (c. 1340–1400)

Roundel from _Parlement of Foules_

"Now welcom somer, with thy sonne softe,
That hast this winters weders over-shake,
And driven awey the longe nightes blake!"

"Seynt Valentyn, that art ful hy on-lofte;—
Thus singen smale foules for thy sake—
  Now welcom somer, with thy sonne softe,
  That hast this wintres weders over-shake.

"Wel han they cause for to gladen ofte,
Sith ech of hem recovered hath his make;
Ful blisful may they singen when they wake;
  No welcom somer, with thy sonne softe,
  That hast this wintres weders over-shake,
  And driven awey the longe nightes blake."

MOTOKIYO (1374–1455)

Chorus from *Kakitsubata: Spirit of the Iris*

The sleeves are white like the snow of the Uno Flower
Dropping their petals in April.
Day comes, the purple flower
    Opens its heart of wisdom,
It fades out of sight by its thought.
The flower soul melts into Buddha.

Translated from the Japanese by Ezra Pound and Ernest Fenollosa

CHRISTOPHER MARLOWE (1564–1593)

"I walked along a stream"

I walked along a stream for pureness rare,
    Brighter than sunshine, for it did acquaint
      The dullest sight with all the glorious prey,
      That in the pebble-paved channel lay.

No molten crystal, but a richer mine,
    Even Nature's rarest alchemy ran there,
Diamonds resolved, and substance more divine,
    Through whose bright gliding current might appear
A thousand naked nymphs, whose ivory shine,
    Enamelling the banks, made them more dear
      Than ever was that glorious palace gate,
      Where the day-shining sun in triumph sat.

Upon this brim the eglantine and rose,
    The tamarisk, olive, and the almond tree,
As kind companions in one union grows,
    Folding their twining arms, as oft we see
Turtle-taught lovers either other close,
    Lending to dullness feeling sympathy.
      And as a costly valance o'er a bed,
      So did their garland tops the brook o'erspread.

Their leaves that differed both in shape and show,
    (Though all were green) yet difference such in green,
Like to the checkered bent of Iris' bow,
    Prided the running main as it had been—

WILLIAM SHAKESPEARE (1564–1616)

Song from *As You Like It* [Act II, Scene 7]

Lord Amiens

Blow, blow, thou winter wind,
Thou art not so unkind
  As man's ingratitude;
Thy tooth is not so keen,
Because thou art not seen,
  Although thy breath be rude.
Heigh-ho! sing heigh-ho!
  unto the green holly.
Most friendship is feigning, most loving
  mere folly:
    Then heigh-ho, the holly!
    This life is most jolly.

Freeze, freeze, thou bitter sky,
That dost not bite so nigh
  As benefits forgot.
Though thou the waters warp,
Thy sting is not so sharp
  As friend rememb'red not.
Heigh-ho! sing heigh-ho!
  unto the green holly.
Most friendship is feigning, most loving
  mere folly:
    Then heigh-ho, the holly!
    This life is most jolly.

JOHN DONNE (1572–1631)

The Sun Rising

Busy old fool, unruly Sun,
Why dost thou thus,
Through windows, and through curtains call on us?
Must to thy motions lovers' seasons run?
Saucy, pedantic wretch, go chide
Late school-boys, and sour prentices,
Go tell Court-huntsmen, that the King will ride,
Call country ants to harvest offices;
Love, all alike, no season knows, nor clime,
Nor hours, days, months, which are the rags of time.

Thy beams so reverend, and strong
Why shouldst thou think?
I could eclipse and cloud them with a wink,
But that I would not lose her sight so long:
If her eyes have not blinded thine,
Look, and to-morrow late, tell me,
Whether both th' Indias of spice and mine
Be where thou left's them, or lie here with me.
Ask for those Kings whom thou saw'st yesterday,
And thou shalt hear, All here in one bed lay.

She's all States, and all Princes, I,
Nothing else is.
Princes do but play us; compar'd to this,
All honour's mimic; all wealth alchemy.
Thou sun art half as happy as we,
In that the world's contracted thus;
Thine age asks ease, and since thy duties be
To warm the world, that's done in warming us.
Shine here to us, and thou art everywhere;
This bed thy centre is, these walls, thy sphere.

CHRISTOPHER SMART (1722–1771)

From *Jubilate Agno*

For I will consider my Cat Jeoffry.
For he is the servant of the Living God, duly and daily serving him.
For at the first glance of the glory of God in the East he
    worships in his way.
For is this done by wreathing his body seven times round with
    elegant quickness.
For then he leaps up to catch the musk, which is the blessing
    of God upon his prayer.
For he rolls upon prank to work it in.
For having done duty and received blessing he begins to
    consider himself.
For this he performs in ten degrees.
For first he looks upon his fore-paws to see if they are clean.
For secondly he kicks up behind to clear away there.
For thirdly he works it upon stretch with the fore-paws extended.
For fourthly he sharpens his paws by wood.
For fifthly he washes himself.
For sixthly he rolls upon wash.
For seventhly he fleas himself, that he may not be interrupted
    upon the beat.
For eighthly he rubs himself against a post.
For ninthly he looks up for his instructions.
For tenthly he goes in quest of food.

. . .

For in his morning orisons he loves the sun and the sun loves him.
For he is of the tribe of Tiger.
For the Cherub Cat is a term of the Angel Tiger.

. . .

For the divine spirit comes about his body to sustain it in
    compleat cat.

JOHANN WOLFGANG VON GOETHE (1749–1832)

From *Faust: Part I*

Ariel
If loving nature gave you wings
and Mind their use proposes,
follow the airy road I take
up to the hill of roses.

Translated from the German by C. F. MacIntyre

GÉRARD DE NERVAL (1808–1855)

Golden Lines

> *What!   Everything is sentient!*
> —Pythagoras

Man, free thinker! do you believe yourself the one alone thinking
In this world where life bursts forth in everything?
Your free will disposes of the forces that you hold
But in all your councils the universe is absent.

Respect in the animal an active intellect:
Each flower is a soul in Nature bloomd forth;
A mystery of love lies conceald in the metal;
"Everything is sentient!"
        Everything has power over your being.

Beware in the blind wall a gaze that watches you:
To matter itself a voice is in-bound . . .
Do not make it serve some impious use!

Often in the obscure being dwells a hidden God;
And like a nascent eye coverd by its lids
A pure spirit grows beneath the skin of stones.

Translated from the French by Robert Duncan

HERMAN MELVILLE (1819–1891)

The Ravaged Villa

In shards the sylvan vases lie,
    Their links of dance undone,
And brambles wither by thy brim,
    Choked fountain of the sun!
The spider in the laurel spins,
    The weed exiles the flower:
And, flung to kiln, Apollo's bust
    Makes lime for Mammon's tower.

CHARLES BAUDELAIRE (1821–1867)

The Ruined Garden

My childhood was only a menacing shower,
cut now and then by hours of brilliant heat.
All the top soil was killed by rain and sleet,
my garden hardly bore a standing flower.

From now on, my mind's autumn! I must take
the field and dress my beds with spade and rake
and restore order to my flooded grounds.
There the rain raised mountains like burial mounds.

I throw fresh seeds out. Who knows what survives?
What elements will give us life and food?
This soil is irrigated by the tides.

Time and nature sluice away our lives.
A virus eats the heart out of our sides,
digs in and multiplies on our lost blood.

Translated from the French by Robert Lowell

STÉPHANE MALLARMÉ (1842–1898)

Sigh

Towards your brow where an autumn dreams
freckled with russet scatterings—
calm sister—and towards the sky,
wandering, of your angelic eye
my soul ascends: thus, white and true,
within some melancholy garden
a fountain sighs toward the Blue!
—Towards October's softened Blue
that pure and pale in the great pools
mirrors its endless lassitude
and, on dead winter where the leaves
wind-strayed in tawny anguish cleave
old furrows, lets the yellow sun
in one long lingering ray crawl on.

Translated from the French by Fredrick Morgan

GERARD MANLEY HOPKINS (1844–1889)

From *The Note-Books*

It is a happy thing that there is no royal road to poetry. The world should know by this time that one cannot reach Parnassus except by flying thither. Yet from time to time more men go up and either perish in its gullies fluttering *excelsior* flags or else come down again with full folios and blank countenances. Yet the old fallacy keeps its ground. Every age has its false alarms.

*

Moonlight hanging or dropping on treetops like blue cobweb.

*

Also the upper sides of little grotted waves turned to the sky have soft pale-coloured cobwebs on them, the under sides green.

*

Note that the beaded oar, dripping, powders or sows the smooth with dry silver drops.

*

The sky minted into golden sequins.
Stars like gold tufts.
—— —— golden bees.
—— —— golden rowels.

ARTHUR RIMBAUD (1854–1891)

Flowers

From a golden step,—among silk cords, green velvets, gray gauzes, and crystal discs that turn black as bronze in the sun, I see the digitalis opening on a carpet of silver filigree, of eyes and hair.

Yellow gold-pieces strewn over agate, mahogany columns supporting emerald domes, bouquets of white satin and delicate sprays of rubies, surround the water-rose.

Like a god with huge blue eyes and limbs of snow, the sea and sky lure to the marble terraces the throng of roses, young and strong.

Translated from the French by Louise Varèse

RAINER MARIA RILKE (1875–1926)

From *Sonnets to Orpheus*

II:5

Flower-muscle of the anemone
slowly opening into the meadow's
morning till in her womb a polyphony
of light from the resounding heavens flows;

flower-muscle, organ of huge infusion,
taut in the still star of the blossom, some-
times fully overcome by wild profusion,
and, like the falling sun about to come

to rest, she barely can become unfurled
to give you her outspreading petal's form,
her will and power of a multiple world!

We violent ones persist. We may perceive
but when? In which life then will we conform
and in the end grow open and receive?

Translated from the German by Willis Barnstone

AKIKO YOSANO (1878–1942)

THREE POEMS

I have the delusion
that you are with me
as I walk through the fields
of flowers, under the moon.

*

Left on the beach
Full of water,
A worn out boat
Reflects the white sky
Of early autumn.

*

Like tiny golden
Birds the gingko leaves scatter
From the tree on the
Hill in the sunset glow.

Translated from the Japanese by Kenneth Rexroth & Ikuko Atsumi

GUILLAME APOLLINAIRE (1880–1918)

Ocean of Earth

To G. de Chirico

I built a house in the middle of the ocean
Its windows are rivers which flow out of my eyes
Octopus stir all around its walls
Listen to the triple beat of their hearts and their beaks which
    tap on the window panes
               Humid house
               Burning house
               Rapid season
               Season which sings
       Airplanes drop eggs
       Watch out for the anchor
Watch out for the ink which they squirt
It's a good thing you came from the sky
The honeysuckle of the sky climbs up
The earthly octopus throb
And then we are closer and closer to being our own gravediggers
Pale octopus of chalky waves O octopus with pale beaks
Around the house there is this ocean which you know
And which is never still

Translated from the French by Roger Shattuck

WILLIAM CARLOS WILLIAMS (1883–1963)

The Yellow Flower

What shall I say, because talk I must?
        That I have found a cure
                for the sick?
I have found no cure
        for the sick   .
                but this crooked flower
which only to look upon
        all men
                are cured. This
is that flower
        for which all men
                sing secretly their hymns
of praise. This
        is that sacred
                flower!
Can this be so?
        A flower so crooked
                and obscure? It is
a mustard flower
        and not a mustard flower,
                a single spray
topping the deformed stem
        of fleshy leaves
                in this freezing weather
under glass.

An ungainly flower and
        an unnatural one,
                in this climate; what
can be the reason
        that it has picked me out
                to hold me, openmouthed,
rooted before this window
        in the cold,

                    my will
drained from me
            so that I have only eyes
                        for these yellow,
twisted petals   .   ?

That the sight,
            though strange to me,
                        must be a common one,
is clear: there are such flowers
            with such leaves
                        native to some climate
which they can call
            their own.

But why the torture
            and the escape through
                        the flower? It is
as if Michelangelo
            had conceived the subject
                        of his *Slaves* from this
—or might have done so.
            And did he not make
                        the marble bloom? I
am sad
            as he was sad
                        in his heroic mood.
But also
            I have eyes
                        that are made to see and if
they see ruin for myself
            and all that I hold
                        dear, they see
also
            through the eyes
                        and through the lips
and tongue the power
            to free myself
                        and speak of it, as

Michelangelo through his hands
          had the same, if greater,
                    power.

Which leaves, to account for,
          the tortured bodies
                    of
the slaves themselves
          and
                    the tortured body of my flower
which is not a mustard flower at all
          but some unrecognized
                    and unearthly flower
for me to naturalize
          and acclimate
                    and choose it for my own.

JULES SUPERVIELLE (1884–1960)

Bear

At the breathless Pole
A bear is turning round and round
A ball whiter
Than snow and as shining.
How can you make him understand
From the depths of this Paris
That this is an old globe,
Ever more and more reduced,
Of a midnight sun.
The bear is so far away
From this closed room.
He is so different
From the familiar beasts
Who pass my door.
The bear, uncomprehending, bends over
His little sun
And tries, bit by bit,
To warm it with his breath
And his dark tongue.
As if he took it
For another chilly bear
Dying inside the ball,
With tight closed eyes.

Translated from the French by Kenneth Rexroth

EZRA POUND (1885–1972)

Canto XLIX

For the seven lakes, and by no man these verses:
Rain; empty river; a voyage,
Fire from frozen cloud, heavy rain in the twilight
Under the cabin roof was one lantern.
The reeds are heavy; bent;
and the bamboos speak as if weeping.

Autumn moon; hills rise about lakes
against sunset
Evening is like a curtain of cloud,
a blur above ripples; and through it
sharp long spikes of cinnamon,
a cold tune amid reeds.
Behind hill the monk's bell
borne on the wind.
Sail passed here in April; may return in October
Boat fades in silver; slowly;
Sun blaze alone on the river.

Where wine flag catches the sunset
Sparse chimneys smoke in the cross light

Comes then snow scur on the river
And a world is covered with jade
Small boat floats like a lanthorn,
The flowing water clots as with cold. And at San Yin
they are a people of leisure.
Wild geese swoop to the sand-bar,
Clouds gather about the hole of the window
Broad water; geese line out with the autumn
Rooks clatter over the fishermen's lanthorns,
A light moves on the north sky line;
where the young boys prod stones for shrimp.
In seventeen hundred came Tsing to these hill lakes.

A light moves on the south sky line.

State by creating riches shd. thereby get into debt?
This is infamy; this is Geryon.
This canal goes still to TenShi
though the old king built it for pleasure

K E I   M E N   RAN   K E I
K I U   M A N   MAN   K E I
JITSU GETSU   K O   KWA
T A N FUKU   TAN   K A I

Sun up; work
sundown; to rest
dig well and drink of the water
dig field; eat of the grain
Imperial power is? and to us what is it?

The fourth; the dimension of stillness.
And the power over wild beasts.

D. H. LAWRENCE (1885–1930)

Hymn of Quetzalcoatl

Naked I come from my Father.
Naked I come from out of the deep, having taken the far way
    round, from heaven where the angels are, and the sons of God.

With the eagle of my right hand down the farthermost sky.
With the serpent of my left hand I travelled the under-earth.
The sky is mine, in my right hand, the earth is mine,
    in my left.
But my heart is the heart my Father gave me, more than the
    heart of a man.

I am Quetzalcoatl, Lord of Life between earth and sky.
All things that rise from earth towards sky in the lift of living
    are mine.
But the heart is my Father's.

The roots are mine, down the dark, moist paths of the snake.
And the branches are mine, in the paths of the sky and the bird.
But the heart invisible belongs to my Father, the Everlasting
    God.

The feet of men and women are mine,
The feet and the legs and the loins, and the bowels of strength
    and of seed are mind.
The serpent of my left-hand darkness shall kiss your feet with
    his mouth,
And put his strength round your ankles, his fire in your legs
    and your loins, his circle of rest in your belly.
For I am Quetzalcoatl, the serpent of the earth's caress.

And I am the eagle of the sky, filling your faces with daylight
And fanning your breasts with my breath
And building my nest of peace in your bosom.
Quetzalcoatl.

H.D. (1887–1961)

THREE POEMS FROM *Sea Garden*

Sea Poppies

Amber husk
fluted with gold,
fruit on the sand
marked with a rich grain,

treasure
spilled near the shrub-pines
to bleach on the boulders:

your stalk has caught root
among wet pebbles
and drift flung by the sea
and grated shells
and split conch-shells.

Beautiful, wide-spread,
fire upon leaf,
what meadow yields
so fragrant a leaf
as your bright leaf?

Sea Violet

The white violet
is scented on its stalk,
the sea-violet
fragile as agate,
lies fronting all the wind
among the torn shells
on the sand-bank.

The greater blue violets
flutter on the hill,
but who would change for these
who would change for these
one root of the white sort?

Violet
your grasp is frail
on the edge of the sand-hill,
but you catch the light—
frost, a star edges with its fire.

Sea Iris

I
Weed, moss-weed,
root tangled in sand,
sea-iris, brittle flower,
one petal like a shell
is broken,
and you print a shadow
like a thin twig.

Fortunate one,
scented and stinging,
rigid myrrh-bud,
camphor-flower,
sweet and salt—you are wind
in our nostrils.

II
Do the murex-fishers
drench you as they pass?
Do your roots drag up color
from the sand?
Have they slipped gold under you—
rivets of gold?

Band of iris-flowers
above the waves,
you are painted blue,
painted like a fresh prow
stained among the salt weeds.

GOTTFRIED BENN (1886–1965)

Epilogue

The drunken torrents are falling—
the blueness is dying now
and the corals are pale as the water
round the island of Palau.

The drunken torrents are broken,
grown alien, to you, to me,
our only possession the silence
of a bone washed clean by the sea.

The floods, the flames, the questions—
till the ashes tell you one day:
"Life is the building of bridges
over rivers that seep away."

Translated from the German by Michael Hamburger

BLAISE CENDRARS (1887–1961)

From Panama or the Adventures of My Seven Uncles

This morning is the first day on earth,
Isthmus
From which you can see all the stars in the sky at one time and
    all forms of vegetation
Marvel of the equatorial mountains,
Only and unique Zone.
There's still the steamboat of the Patterson *Starch*
The colored initials of the Atlantic and Pacific Tea Company
The Los Angeles Limited that leaves at 10:02 to arrive the
    third day and that is the only train in the world to carry a
    barbershop
The Grand Trunk eclipses and the little cars for children
That teach you the ABC of life under the switch of the sirens
    of departure.
Toyo Kisen Kaisha
I have bread and cheese
A clean collar
And poetry dates from today.

Translated from the French by John Dos Passos

ROBINSON JEFFERS (1887–1962)

From *Cawdor*

                    The wind had shifted before
     dawn and grooved itself
A violent channel from east of south, the slant of the coast;
     the house-roof groaned, the planted cypresses
Flung broken boughs over the gables and all the lee slope
     of the gorge was carpeted green
With the new growth and little twigs of the redwoods.
     They bowed themselves at last, the redwoods, not shaken
By common storms, bowed themselves over; their voice and not
     the ocean's was the great throat of the gorge
That roared it full, taking all the storm's other
Noises like little fish in a net.

                    . . .

                    In the afternoon the wind
Fell, and the spray in the wind waxed into rain.
The men came home, they boarded the broken window.
The rain increased all night. At dawn a high sea-bird,
If any had risen so high, watching the hoary light
Creep down to sea, under the cloud-streams, down
The many canyons the great sea-wall of coast
Is notched with like a murderer's gun-stock, would have seen
Each canyon's creek-mouth smoke its mud-brown torrent
Into the shoring gray; and as the light gained
Have seen the whole wall gleam with a glaze of water.

SAINT-JOHN PERSE (1887–1975)

From *Anabasis*

We shall not dwell forever in these yellow lands, our pleasance. . . .

The Summer vaster than the Empire hangs over the tables of space several terraces of climate. The huge earth rolls on its surface overflowing its pale embers under the ashes—. Sulphur color, honey color of immortal things, the whole grassy earth taking light from the straw of last winter—and from the green sponge of a lone tree the sky draws its violet juices.

A place glittering with mica! Not a pure grain in the wind's barbs. And light like oil.—From the crack of my eye to the level of the hills I join myself, I know the stones gillstained, the swarms of silence in the hives of light; and my heart gives heed to a family of locusts. . . .

Like milch-camels, gentle beneath the shears and sewn with mauve scars, let the hills march forth under the scheme of the harvest sky—let them march in silence over the pale incandescence of the plain; and kneel at last, in the smoke of dreams, there where the peoples annihilate themselves in the dead powder of earth.

These are the great quiet lines that disperse in the fading blue of doubtful vines. The earth here and there ripens the violets of storm; and these sandsmokes that rise over dead river courses, like the skirts of centuries on their route. . . .

Lower voice for the dead, lower voice by day. Such gentleness in the heart of man, can it fail to find its measure? . . . 'I speak to you, my soul!—my soul darkened by the horse smell!' And several great land birds, voyaging westwards, make good likeness of our sea birds.

In the east of so pale a sky, like a holy place sealed by the blind man's linen, calm clouds arrange themselves, where the cancers of camphor and horn revolve. . . . Smoke which a breath of wind claims from us! the earth poised tense in its insect barbs, the earth is brought to bed of wonders! . . .

And at noon, when the jujuba tree breaks the tombstone,

man closes his lids and cools his neck in the ages. . . .
Horsetramplings of dreams in the place of dead powders, O vain
ways a breath sweeps smoking toward us! where find, where
find, the warriors who shall watch the streams in their nuptials?

At the sound of great waters on march over the earth, all the
salt of the earth shudders in dream. And sudden, ah sudden,
what would these voices with us? Levy a wilderness of mirrors on
the boneyard of streams, let them appeal in the course of ages!
Raise stones to my fame, raise stones to silence; and to guard
these places, cavalcades of green bronze on the great causeways!
. . .

(The shadow of a great bird falls on my face.)

Translated from the French by T. S. Eliot

FERNANDO PESSOA (1888–1935)

From **The Keeper of the Flocks**

Rather the flying bird, leaving no trace
Than the going beast
Marking the earth with his track.

The bird flies by and forgets
(As is only right). The beast
Where he no longer is
(And is therefore no use)
Marks that he was there before
(Which is also no use).

For to remember is to betray
Nature, since the nature of yesterday
Is not nature.
What has been, is nothing.
Remembering
Is failure to see.

Move on, bird, move on, teach me
To move on.

Translated from the Portuguese by Thomas Merton

GIUSEPPE UNGARETTI (1888–1970)

The Island

On a shore where evening was forever
Of woods enrapt and ancient, he descended,
And advanced
And the sound of wings recalled him,
Sound unfettered from the shrill
Heartbeat of the torrid water,
And behind a larva
(Languishing, reflowering);
Climbing on anew, he saw
It was a nymph, slumbering
Erect entwined about an elm

Wandering in his self from semblance
Unto true flame, reached a meadow
Where the shadow thickened in
The eyes of virgins as
Evening at the foot of olive-trees;
The boughs distilled
A lazy rain of arrows,
Here sheep did drowse
Beneath the sleek warmth,
Others browsed
The luminous coverlet;
The hands of the shepherd were a glass
Smoothed by faint fever.

Translated from the Italian by Allen Mandelbaum

JEAN COCTEAU (1889–1963)

From The Laic Mystery

A great artist is inhuman, vegetable, bestial. If he tries to speak his attempts upset us. Stravinsky in the "Sacre" is a growing tree. The Stravinsky of "Histoire du Soldat," the "Serenade," "Oedipus Rex" is the tree that tries to speak and that does speak. Chirico always speaks. He often speaks by means of ventriloquism. Sometimes he speaks alone. Then he relapses. Nothing is more touching than an animal trying to regain the secret of human speech which it has discovered and then lost.

Translated from the French by Olga Rudge

BORIS PASTERNAK (1890–1960)

Improvisation

A flock of keys I had feeding out of my hand,
To clapping of wings and croaking and feathery fight;
On tiptoe I stood and stretched out my arm, and the sleeve
Rolled up, so I felt at my elbow the nudging of night.

And the dark. And a pond in the dark, and the lapping of waves.
And the birds of the species I-love-you that others deny
Would be killed, so it seemed, before the savage black beaks,
The strong and the strident, were ever to falter and die.

And a pond. And the dark. And festive the palpitant flares
From pipkins of midnight pitch. And the boat's keel gnawed
By the wave. And always the greedy noise of the birds
Who fighting over the elbow fluttered and cawed.

The gullets of dams were agurgle, gulping the night.
And the mother birds, if the fledglings on whom they dote
Were not to be fed, would kill, so it seemed, before
The roulades would die in the strident, the crooked throat.

Translated from the Russian by Babette Deutsch

HUGH MACDIARMID (1892–1978)

From On a Raised Beach

to James H. Whyte

All is lithogenesis – or lochia,
Carpolite fruit of the forbidden tree,
Stones blacker than any in the Caaba,
Cream-coloured caen-stone, chatoyant pieces,
Celadon and corbeau, bistre and beige,
Glaucous, hoar, enfouldered, cyathiform,
Making mere faculae of the sun and moon,
I study you glout and gloss, but have
No cadrans to adjust you with, and turn again
From optik to haptik and like a blind man run
My fingers over you, arris by arris, burr by burr,
Slickensides, truité, rugas, foveoles,
Bringing my aesthesis in vain to bear,
An angle-titch to all your corrugations and coigns,
Hatched foraminous cavo-rilievo of the world,
Deictic, fiducial stones. Chiliad by chiliad
What bricole piled you here, stupendous cairn?
What artist poses the Earth écorché thus,
Pillar of creation engouled in me?
What eburnation augments you with men's bones,
Every energumen an Endymion yet?
All the other stones are in this haecceity it seems,
But where is the Christophanic rock that moved?
What Cabirian song from this catasta comes?

. . .

No heavier and colder and quieter then,
No more motionless, do stones lie
    In death than in life to all men.

VINCENTE HUIDOBRO (1893–1948)

Relativity of Spring

You can't do anything about May evenings
Sometimes night comes loose in your hands
And I know your eyes are the end of night

At eight in the morning all the leaves are born
We'll have fruit in place of all those stars

When you go away you lock up the landscape
And no one has tended the sheep by the shore

Spring is relative like a rainbow
It could just as well be a parasol
A parasol over a sigh at noon

Rain puts out the sun

Transalpine parasol or maybe insular
Relative spring triumphal arch above an eyelash
To the right everything's calm and in our path
Like a cushion the dove is lukewarm

Maritime spring
The ocean of May completely green
The ocean remains our private garden
And the waves push up like ferns

I want that wave on the horizon
The only laurel for my brow

In the depths of my mirror the universe comes loose
You can't do anything about evening being born

Translated from the Spanish by Michael Palmer

From **Childhood**

The old elmtrees flock round the tiled farmstead; their silverbel-lied leaves dance in the wind. Beneath their shade, in the corner of the Green, is a pond. In winter it is full of water, green with weeds: in Spring a lily will open there.

The ducks waddle in the mud and sail in circles round the pond, or preen their feathers on the bank.

But in Summer the pond is dry, and its bed is glossy and baked by the sun, a beautiful soft colour like the skins of the moles they catch and crucify on the stable doors.

On the green the fowls pick grains, or chatter and fight. Their yellows, whites and browns, the metallic lustre of their darker feathers, and the crimson splash of their combs make an ever-changing pattern on the grass.

They drink with spasmodic upreaching necks by the side of the well.

Under the stones by the well live green lizards curious to our eyes.

The path from the well leads to the garden door set in the high wall whereon grow plums and apricots. The door is deep and narrow and opens on to paths bordered with box-hedges; one path leads through the aromatic currant bushes, beneath the plum trees, to the lawn where grows the wonder of our day-dreams, the monkey's puzzle-tree. On the other side of the lawn three fir trees rise sharply to the sky, their dark shades homing a few birds.

Beyond is the orchard, and down its avenues of mould-smitten trees the path leads to the paddocks, with their mushrooms and fairy-rings, and to the flatlands that stretch to the girding hills.

CHARLES REZNIKOFF (1894–1976)

From Autobiography: Hollywood

VII.
I look at the opaque red of the passion-flower coldly
and at these bright odorless flowers
that grow so closely. The poppies are still most beautiful
(that grew in the fields before any gardener)
through whose yellow translucent petals
the sun shines
as they stand straight on the slender stems,
native to the soil and sun—
a bright democracy, a company yet each alone.

IX. *Rainy Season*
It has been raining for three days.
The faces of the giants
on the billboards
still smile,
but the gilt has been washed from the sky:
we see the iron world.

X.
The cold wind and black fog and the noise of the sea.

XIV.
I would be the rock
about which the water is
flowing; and I would be the water flowing
about the rock.
And am both and neither—
being flesh.

KENJI MIYAZAWA (1896–1933)

The Great Power Line Pole

rain and clouds drift to the ground
susuki-grass red ears washed
fields fresh and live
and the great power line pole of Hanamaki
sparrows on a hundred insulators
then off to pillage a ricefield
whish whish whish whish flying
light of rain and cloud
and nimbly sweeping back to the hundred insulators
at the fork in the Hanamaki road
sparrows

Translated from the Japanese by Gary Snyder

EUGENIO MONTALE (1896–1981)

After the Rain

On the wet sand ideograms appear
like a hen's claws. I look back but see
neither bird sanctuaries nor shelters.
A tired or perhaps a lame duck
may have passed. I wouldn't be able to decipher
that language even if I were Chinese.
One gust of wind will be enough to cancel it.
It isn't true that Nature is mute.
It speaks at random and the only hope is
it doesn't bother too much about us.

Translated from the Italian by G. Singh

JOHN WHEELWRIGHT (1897–1940)

Seed Pods

for Louise Damon

Where the small heads of violets
are shrunk to smaller skulls,
in meadows where the mind forgets
its bull fights and its bulls;
the dust of violet or rose
relinquishes its scent
and carries with it where it blows
a lessening remnant
of heresies in equipoise
and balanced argument
with which the mind would have refleshed
the flower's skeleton,
but that it found itself enmeshed
in the web of oblivion.
Therefore, when Gabriel sound the horn
and dust rise through the ground,
our flesh shall turn, on our last morn
fleshless as the horn's sound.

FEDERICO GARCÍA LORCA (1898-1936)

Casida of the Dark Doves

Through the branches of the laurel
I saw two dark doves.
The one was the sun,
the other the moon.
Little neighbors, I said to them,
where is my tomb?
In my tail, said the sun.
In my throat, said the moon.
And I who was walking
with the earth at my belt
saw two eagles of marble
and a naked girl.
The one was the other
and the girl was no one.
Little eagles, I said to them,
where is my tomb?
In my tail, said the sun,
in my throat, said the moon.
Through the branches of the laurel
I saw two naked doves.
The one was the other
and both were no one.

Translated from the Spanish by W. S. Merwin

JIŘÍ WOLKER (1900–1924)

Pokora: Humility

I'll grow smaller and smaller
Till I'm the smallest thing on earth.
On an early morning, in a summer meadow
I'll stretch my hand to the smallest flower
And hide my face in it, whispering:
On you, little child, without shoes or clothes,
Heaven leans its hand
In a flashing drop of dew
So that its giant sky
Shan't break into pieces.

*Translated from the Czech (or from Gustav Janouch's German transla-
tion) by Goronwy Rees*

BASIL BUNTING (1900–1985)

From *First Book of Odes*

3

To Peggy Mullett

I am agog for foam. Tumultuous come
with teeming sweetness to the bitter shore
tidelong unrinsed and midday parched and numb
with expectation. If the bright sky bore
with endless utterance of a single blue
unphrased, its restless immobility
infects the soul, which must decline into
an anguished and exact sterility
and waste away: then how much more the sea
trembling with alteration must perfect
our loneliness by its hostility.
The dear companionship of its elect
deepens our envy. Its indifference
haunts us to suicide. Strong memories
of sprayblown days exasperate impatience
to brief rebellion and emphasise
the casual impotence we sicken of.
But when mad waves spring, braceletted with foam,
towards us in the angriness of love
crying a strange name, tossing as they come
repeated invitations in the gay
exuberance of unexplained desire,
we can forget the sad splendour and play
at willfulness until the gods require
renewed inevitable hopeless calm
and the foam dies and we again subside
into our catalepsy, dreaming foam,
while the dry shore awaits another tide.

Nature and Free Animals

I will forgive you everything,
But what you have done to my Dogs
I will not forgive.
You have taught them the sickness of your mind
And the sicknesses of your body
You have taught them to be servile
To hang servilely upon your countenance
To be dependent touching and entertaining
To have rights to be wronged
And wrongs to be righted.
You have taught them to be protected by a Society.
This I will not forgive,
Saith the Lord.
Well, God, it's all very well to talk like this
And I dare say it's all very fine
And Nature and Free Animals
Are all very fine,
Well all I can say is
If you wanted it like that
You shouldn't have created me
Not that I like it very much
And now that I'm on the subject I'll say,
What with Nature and Free Animals on the one side
And you on the other,
I hardly know I'm alive.

SHIMPEI KUSANO (1903–1988)

Monologue of a Hibernating Frog

sleet   or snow?
feels good it soaks into.
my body wet.
mistily moistened.
snow   or cold rain?
acanthus rooting above me gone bad for the cold?
or those withered leaves suffering heavy snow?
what's that faint sound coming on?
a jet?
or a big truck?
like electric massage feels good.
never get hungry.
underground this may be hell.
I think hell is fine.
the dreams I dream always wrapped in a rose mist.
meanwhile spring arrives and. cool-like.
into the dazzling light and air I creep up but.
that's what makes me smile with all my eyes.

Translated by Cid Corman and Sususmu Kamaike

The Infinite Horses

I have seen them asleep on the grass,
mirroring themselves in the fields;
seen them furious, on their knees,
like haughty gods, all white,
dressed in ribbons, savage
with manes flying like the loose hair
of legended sirens on the shores.
Vile vipers have dreamt of them,
reeds and bedded mothers
keep them closed in the palms.
Trembling they foretell battles,
like the beat of their trotting hoofs,
like applause thundering in a vast theater.
They have seen wounds bleeding into the clay,
died among flowers, in the mire,
intimates of birds and vermin.
They draw near bearing armed men,
approach on their backs vile tyrants,
dressed in blood and purple.
I shall remember implacable horses:
Russian trappings; the Przewalski;
the names of the hundred and twenty
Roman horses, chiseled in marble;
at the Olympus of Dionus of Argus,
with a hard penumbra aphrodisiac on
their bronze flanks, the horse
most favored by the others
was that of Altis; he who was so loved
by Semiramis, the queen of Asia;
those who tasted with blessed transports—
long before the Chinese tasted them—
green tea from those inspired leaves;
that horse created by Virgil
whose benign and virtuous shadow was gifted

with the power to heal all horses.
I shall remember in an orange sky,
horses so left in shadow,
concernedly bringing lovers together
in peaceful grottoes from a distance.

Translated from the Spanish by William Carlos Williams

LOUIS ZUKOFSKY (1904–1978)

FOUR POEMS

From *Anew*

21
Can a mote of sunlight defeat its purpose
When thought shows it to be deep or dark?

See sun, and think shadow.

From *Chloride of Lime and Charcoal*

3
How sweet is the sun, is the sun
How sweet is the sun
With the birds, with the summer months
                    the notes of a run
How sweet, sweet is the sun.

You ask what I can do—
My name is Jackie
I am Jack-of-all-trades:
Homer—the carpenter—
Did you write that book?
Is your fir squared
                    and its end true?

How sweet is the sun, is the sun
How sweet is the sun
With the birds, with the summer months
                    the notes of a run
How sweet, sweet is the sun.

From *Barely and widely*

3
The green leaf that will outlast the winter
      because sheltered in the open:
the wall, transverse, and diagonal ribs
      of the privet that pocket air
                  around the leaf inside them
      and cover but with walls of wind:
it happens wind colors like glass shelter,
            as the light's aire from a vault
            which has a knob of sun.

From *80 Flowers*

Artemisia

Art to me's hear stellary
honor never translated my sum
pauper in aerie white *dusty-miller*
feltsmooth *lad's love* disc-buttons dull gold
neume nod grace discord concord
a breath *beach-wormwood suthern wude*
brush cottony *sightwort* booklice blur
old eyes-iris evergreen retainers sun

KENNETH REXROTH (1905–1982)

From **The Dragon and the Unicorn**

The heart's mirror hangs in the void.
Vision blossoms in the night
Like stars opening in the brain.
Jehovah created the world
In six days. The Bible does not
Mention the nights. He holds the
Creation of the night in
Concealment for His own ends.
There is no reality
Except that of experience
And experience is the
Conversation of persons.

. . .

The sun enters the second
Moon of Autumn. The dove turns
To a hawk. Dew becomes hoarfrost.

. . .

As long as we are lost
In the world of purpose
We are not free. I sit
In my ten foot square hut.
The birds sing. The bees hum.
The leaves sway. The water
Murmurs over the rocks.
The canyon shuts me in.
If I moved, Bashō's frog
Would splash in the pool.
All Summer long the gold
Laurel leaves fell through space.
Today I was aware

Of a maple leaf floating
On the pool. In the night
I stare into the fire.
Once I saw fire cities,
Towns, palaces, wars
Heroic adventures,
In the campfires of youth.
Now I see only fire.
My breath moves quietly.
The stars move overhead.
In the clear darkness
Only a small red glow
Is left in the ashes.
On the table lies a cast
Snakeskin and an uncut stone.

. . .

It is the dark of the moon.
Late at night, the end of Summer,
The Autumn constellations
Glow in the arid heaven.
The air smells of cattle, hay,
And dust. In the old orchard
The pears are ripe. The trees
Have sprouted from old rootstocks
And the fruit is inedible.
As I pass them I hear something
Rustling and grunting and turn
My light into the branches.
Two raccoons with acrid pear
Juice and saliva drooling
From their mouths, stare back at me,
Their eyes deep sponges of light.
They know me and do not run
Away. Coming up the road
Through the black oak shadows, I
See ahead of me, glinting
Everywhere from the dusty

Gravel, tiny points of cold
Blue light, like the sparkle of
Iron snow. I suspect what it is,
And kneel to see. Under each
Pebble and oak leaf is a
Spider, her eyes shining at
Me with my reflected light
Across immeasurable distance.

RENÉ CHAR (1907–1988)

Courbet: The Stone Breakers

Sand straw live softly softly take the wine
Gather the down-drifting dovecot feathers
Parch with the avid water-channel
Stay girls barefoot going
Pierce their chrysalids
Drink lightly carelessly the well suffered blood

We devour the grey fire's pest among the stones
While in the village they plot and plan
The best place still for men is the ruined roads
The tomatoes in the garden are borne to us on the twilight air
And of our women's next spite forgetfulness
And the smart of thirst aching in our knees

Sons this night our labor of dust
Will be visible in the sky
Already the oil rises from the lead again.

Translated from the French by Samuel Beckett

GUILLEVIC (1907–1997)

Dwellings

I have dwelt in the blackbird.
I believe I know
how the blackbird wakes, how he wants
to say the light, still part of
darkness, a few colors,
their heavy play across
that red he encounters within him.

Within the wheatstalks
I have sustained verticality.

With the pond I have wavered
towards sleep that is always nearby.

I have lived in a flower.
There I have seen the sun
approach to study the flower
and spend much time
inciting it to dare its own limits.

I have lived in fruit
that dreamed of enduring.

I have lived
in eyes that thought of smiling.

Translated from the French by Denise Levertov

GEORGE OPPEN (1908–1984)

The Forms of Love

Parked in the fields
All night
So many years ago,
We saw
A lake beside us
When the moon rose.
I remember

Leaving that ancient car
Together. I remember
Standing in the white grass
Beside it. We groped
Our way together
Downhill in the bright
Incredible light

Beginning to wonder
Whether it could be lake
Or fog
We saw, our heads
Ringing under the stars we walked
To where it would have wet our feet
Had it been water

ARUN MITRA (1909–2000)

The Song of the Harvest

Leaves of the spring and summer storms
make me eager and expectant.
The murmur of falling rain
or the morning music of autumn permeates my being.
The village in the late winter
brings a strange music to my ears.

Whenever I touch the earth I feel
I have returned to my old world.
In your body I seek the throb of growing roots.
In my embrace the vastness of the world narrows down.
The expectancy of your lips thrusts up with the urge of life
in a thousand hints and suggestions.
A suspense hovers over all my world.

When we whisper softly to one another
its fragrance fills the whole world:
The distant horizon comes near in my hopes.
When I look at your face
I believe words can be full of life like flowers.

We are people of the land of rivers.
Its heart is wide open to us
and to it we return.
This is why I love you.
Here we can be intimate like the spreading turf
or like the gentle rain.
Here we can conquer the fear that dries the sap in the roots,
the rigors of the desert that dry up the clouds
and become one with the future.
All strangeness and familiarity we tread beneath our feet—
even our sufferings make rich the days.
In vast rivers we float our songs;
the plains thrill and burst into music.

We seek to drown ourselves in the depths of our eyes.
We want to renew ourselves like the harvest.
Sometimes underneath the evening star
sometimes in the early dawn when the birds awake
sometimes in the middle of the day, in the deserted house
I draw you to me and push aside all outside whisperings.
In deep human love
I deny the memories of a failing past.
I call on you to blossom like a new twig.
I say:
Be like the sheaves of new corn;
the flowers of the golden mustard.
I say:
Embrace me in your deep murmur.

Translated from the Bengali by Humayun Kabir et al.

CHARLES OLSON (1910–1970)

Spring

The dogwood
lights up the day

The April moon
flakes the night

Birds, suddenly,
are a multitude

The flowers are ravined
by bees, the fruit blossoms

are thrown to the ground, the wind
the rain forces everything. Noise—

even the night is drummed
by whippoorwills, and we get

as busy, we plow, we move,
we break out, we love. The secret

which got lost neither hides
nor reveals itself, it shows forth

tokens. And we rush
to catch up. The body

whips the soul. In its great desire
it demands the elixir

In the roar of spring,
transmutations. Envy

drags herself off. The fault of the body and the soul
—that they are not one—

the matutinal cock clangs
and singleness: we salute you

season of no bungling

PABLO NERUDA (1910–1973)

The Infinite One

Do you see these hands? They have measured
the earth, they have separated
minerals and cereals,
they have made peace and war,
they have demolished the distances
of all the seas and rivers,
and yet,
when they move over you,
little one,
grain of wheat, swallow,
they can not encompass you,
they are weary seeking
the twin doves
that rest or fly in your breast,
they travel the distances of your legs,
they coil in the light of your waist.
For me you are a treasure more laden
with immensity than the sea and its branches
and you are white and blue and spacious like
the earth at vintage time.
In that territory,
from your feet to your brow,
walking, walking, walking,
I shall spend my life.

Translated from the Spanish by Donald D. Walsh

KENNETH PATCHEN (1911–1972)

All is Safe . . .

Flow, water, the blue water
Little birds of foam
Singing on thee
O flow, water, blue water
Little stars falling asleep
To thy tossing
O flow, water, the blue water
What matters any sorrow
It is lost in thee

Little times, little men
What matters
They are safe in thee
O
Flow, water, blue water
All is safe in thee
Little birds
The shadows of maidens
O safe in thy singing

TENNESSEE WILLIAMS (1911–1983)

From A Separate Poem

The day turns holy as though a god moved through it,
wanderingly, unknowing and unknown,
led by the sky as a child is led by its mother.

But the sky of an island is a wandering sky.
It seems bewildered sometimes, it seems bewildered as we are
since the loss of our island.
Oh, yes, we've lost our island.
                            Time took it from us,
snatched it out of our hands as a fresh runner snatches
out of a spent runner's hand
the bit of white cloth to continue.
                            Still
we live on the island, but more as visitors,
than as residents, now.
                            Still we remember
things our island has taught us: how to let the sky go
        (as a bit of white cloth to continue)
and other things of a smaller, more intimate nature.
Our island has been a school in which we were backward pupils
but, finally, learning a little, such as:
lies die, but truth doesn't live except in the truth of our island
which is a truth that wanders, led by the sky
as a child is led by its mother, and the sky wanders, too.

WILLIAM EVERSON (1912–1994)

We in the Fields

Dawn and a high film; the sun burned it;
But noon had a thick sheet, and the clouds coming,
The low rain-bringers, trooping in from the north,
From the far cold fog-breeding seas, the womb of the storms.
Dusk brought a wind and the sky opened:
All down the west the broken strips lay snared in the light,
Bellied and humped and heaped on the hills.
The set sun threw the blaze up;
The sky lived redly, banner on banner of far-burning flame,
From south to the north the furnace door wide and the smoke
    rolling.
We in the fields, the watchers from the burnt slope,
Facing the west, facing the bright sky, hopelessly longing
    to know the red beauty—
But the unable eyes, the too-small intelligence,
The insufficient organs of reception
Not a thousandth part enough to take and retain.
We stared, and no speaking, and felt the deep loneness of
    incomprehension.
The flesh must turn cloud, the spirit, air,
Transformation to sky and the burning,
Absolute oneness with the west and the down sun.
But we, being earth-stuck, watched from the fields,
Till the rising rim shut out the light;
Till the sky changed, the long wounds healed;
Till the rain fell.

DELMORE SCHWARTZ (1913–1966)

Phoenix Lyrics

I
If nature is life, nature is death:
It is winter as it is spring:
Confusion is variety, variety
And confusion in everything
Make experience the true conclusion
Of all desire and opulence,
All satisfaction and poverty.

II
When a hundred years had passed nature seemed to man
        a clock
Another century sank away and nature seemed a jungle
        in a rock
And now that nature has become a ticking and hidden
        bomb how we must mock
Newton, Democritus, the Deity
The heart's ingenuity and the mind's infinite
    uncontrollable
            insatiable curiosity.

III
Purple black cloud at sunset: it is late August
and the light begins to look cold, and as we look,
listen and look, we hear the first drums of autumn.

MURIEL RUKEYSER (1913–1980)

From **Elegy in Joy**

We tell beginnings : for the flesh and the answer,
for the look, the lake in the eye that knows,
for the despair that flows down in widest rivers,
cloud of home;   and also the green tree of grace,
all in the leaf, in the love that gives us ourselves.

The word of nourishment passes through the women,
soldiers and orchards rooted in constellations,
white towers, eyes of children:
saying in time of war What shall we feed?
I cannot say the end.

Nourish beginnings, let us nourish beginnings.
Not all things are blest, but the
seeds of all things are blest.
The blessing is in the seed.

This moment, this seed, this wave of the sea, this look, this
    instant of love.
Years over wars and an imagining of peace.   Or the
    expiation journey
toward peace which is many wishes flaming together,
fierce pure life, the many-living home.
Love that gives us ourselves, in the world known to all
new techniques for the healing of the wound,
and the unknown world.   One life, or the faring stars.

JOHN FREDERICK NIMS (1913–1999)

From The Six-Cornered Snowflake

❋
We
dream
in neurons.
Form lost in forms,
❋ a blizzard of data blinds our monitors. ❋
Today, more knowing, we know less. But know
less more minutely. A schoolboy could
dazzle poor Kepler with his chemistry,
chat of molecular bonds, how H:ö:H
freezes to crystal, the six struts
magnetized by six hydrogen nuclei
(so goes a modern Magnificat to snow)
its six electrical terminals alluring
a bevy of sprightly molecules from out of
❋ weather's nudge and buffeting, the tips ❋
culling identical
windfalls
of fey
air
❋

NICANOR PARRA (b. 1914)

The Error Consisted

In believing that the Earth was ours
When the reality of the situation
Is that we
        belong
                to the
                        Earth
Clara Sandoval used to tell us

Translated from the Spanish by Liz Werner

DYLAN THOMAS (1914–1953)

We See Rise the Secret Wind

We see rise the secret wind behind the brain,
The sphinx of light sit on the eyes,
The code of stars translate in heaven,
A secret night descends between
The skull, the cells, the cabinned ears
Holding for ever the dead moon.

A shout went up to heaven like a rocket,
Woe from the rabble of the blind
Adorners of the city's forehead,
Gilders of the streets, the rabble hand
Saluting the busy brotherhood
Of rod and wheel that wake the dead.

A city godhead, turbine moved, steel sculptured,
Glitters in the electric streets;
A city saviour, in the orchard
Of lamp-posts and high-volted fruits,
Speaks a steel gospel to the wretched
Wheel-winders and fixers of bolts.

We hear rise the secret wind behind the brain,
The secret voice cry in our ears,
The city gospel shout to heaven.
Over the electric godhead grows
One God, more mighty than the sun.
The cities have not robbed our eyes.

JAMES LAUGHLIN (1914–1997)

In the Snow

The track of the ermine
the track of the mouse

tracks of a deer in the
snow and my track that

wanders and hesitates
doubling and crossing

itself stops to burrow
and circles trees this

track I made twists like
the veins in a leaf or a

crack in a mirror and it
cries seems to cry cries

to the sun cries sun sun
touch and burn cries sun

touch and save cries to
the sun—and then snow

falls covering everything
new snow covers my track

covers the track of the
ermine mouse and deer.

Four Poplars

As if it were behind itself this line runs
chasing itself through the horizontal confines
west, forever fugitive
where it tracks itself it scatters

—as this same line
raised in a glance
transforms all of its letters
into a diaphanous column
breaking into an untouched
unheard, untasted, yet imagined
flower of vowels and consonants

—as this line that never stops writing itself
and before completion gathers itself
never ceasing to flow, but flowing upward:

the four poplars.

　　　　　Drawing breath
from the empty heights and there below,
doubled in a pond turned sky,
the four are a single poplar
and are none.

　　　　　Behind, a flaming foliage
dies out—the afternoon's adrift—
other poplars, now ghostly tatters,
interminably undulate,
interminably keep still.

Yellow slips into pink,
night insinuates itself in the violet.

Between the sky and the water
there is a blue and green band:
sun and aquatic plants,
a calligraphy of flames
written by the wind.
It is a reflection suspended in another.

Passages: a moment's blink.
The world loses shape,
it is an apparition, it is four poplars,
four purple melodies.

Fragile branches creep up the trunks.
They are a bit of light and a bit of wind.
A motionless shimmer. With my eyes
I hear them murmur words of air.

Silence runs off with the creek,
comes back with the sky.

What I see is real:
four weightless poplars
planted in vertigo.
Fixed points that rush
down, rush up,
rush to the water of the sky of the marsh
in a wispy, tenuous travail
while the world sails into darkness.

Pulse-beat of last light:
fifteen beleaguered minutes
Claude Monet watches from a boat.

The sky immerses itself in the water,
the water drowns,
the poplar is an opal thrust:
this world is not solid.

Between being and non-being the grass wavers,
the elements become lighter,
outlines shade over,
glimmers, reflections, reverberations,
flashes of forms and presences,
image mist, eclipse:
what I see, we are: mirages.

Translated from the Spanish by Eliot Weinberger

C. H. SISSON (1914–2003)

The Sow's Ear

The sow's ear
Is now more valuable than the silk purse,
Nature than art, the silk-worm than the silk.
The breast now swelling with tomorrow's milk
Signifies hope, and the young eyes averse
From any fear.

So the bud too
Promises silently the future flower;
The chrysalis in winter in its sleep
Marks out the place of wings. Nature may keep
Her undertakings in another hour:
So may not you.

The race which came
To eve by Adam has another plan:
Corrupt the garden and destroy the seed.
Its work is almost done, and former need
Translated into all that pleases man.
The hunted game

Shrinks and the leaf
That once hid Adam's shame dies on the tree.
The rivers die, the seas are empty now.
The fish lie stranded and upon the bough
The fruit is only shadow, and we see
Our time is brief.

THOMAS MERTON (1915–1968)

Hare's Message (Hottentot)

One day Moongod wanted to send a message to man. Hare volunteered to go to man as Moongod's messenger. "Go tell men," said Moon, "that they shall all rise again the way I also rise after each dying." But Hare the messenger deceived man, changing the heavenly message to one of earth. "You must die," he said, "just as I do." Then Moon cursed Hare. And the Nagama must now never eat Hare's meat. They do not eat Hare the runner for the runner is death.

ROBERT LAX (1915–2000)

Tiger

a tiger
is like a
butterfly,
thought
the
tiger,

here today,
gone tomorrow

he is like a
bird—a hawk,
forever
vigilant

he is even
a little
like an
elephant,

ponderous
& basically
gentle.

not too
gentle,

said a
younger
tiger.

i only meant it

as a metaphor,
said the old one,

a tiger is like
a number of
things.

JOHANNES BOBROWSKI (1917–1965)

The Hawk

"Wing,
bird-wing,
arch in the smoke, light –
fall out of sleep,
arrow, sweep over the
river, fly, a strip of rain,
in the light of the banks."

Water-haze, white,
which darkens
the feather. Wind,
which roughens me. Storm
across the plains. Crumbling with weeds,
evening, water-bushes.

"Under the drag of the air
outside dreamless he travels
with staring eyes, the killer
travels with the wind."

Oh, borne up
over the tree
of dusk, high in the light,
the rushing silence – yet still
light, sea, wave-song, the sails
over the depth, upon the seaweeds'
shadow, I travel through the light –
travel with the storm,
higher, he hunts with the scourge,
night-storm, the cutting knife of luck
between his teeth.

Translated from the German by Ruth and Matthew Mead

SATURNO MONTANARI (1918–1941)

Stagione di Fiore

Time of almonds in flower
and songs half spoken;
walnut's bough now
keeps sun off threshed oats.

Time comes again
from the shepherd's pens:
shy flowers in wind
each year, thus, with no pain;

Renews the rillets, and dews.
White thorn, darkens in pine
with new spikes, a heaven of birds
sing to line.

Comes joy's season, that does no ill
for our brother the sun, aloft,
keeps it too languid and still
for any evil.

Translated from the Italian by Ezra Pound

WILLIAM BRONK (1918–1999)

Aspects of the World Like Coral Reefs

In the spring woods, how good it is to see
again the trees, old company,
how they have withstood the winter, their girth.

By gradual actions, how the gross earth
gathers around us and grows real, is there,
as though it were really there, and is good.

Certain stars, of stupendous size, are said
to be such and such distances away,—
oh, farther than the eyes alone would ever see.

Thus magnified, the whole evidence
of our senses is belied. For it is not
possible for miles to add miles to miles

forever, not even if expressed as the speed of light.
The fault lies partly in the idea of miles.
It is absurd to describe the world in sensible terms.

How good that even so, aspects of the world
that are real, or seem to be real, should rise like reefs
whose rough agglomerate smashes the sea.

MURIEL SPARK (1918–2006)

Flower Into Animal

This is the pain that sea anemones bear
in the fear of aberration but willfully
aspiring to respire in another
more difficult way, and turning
flower into animal interminably.

It is a pain to choke with, when the best
of a species gets lost somewhere.
Different, indifferent pain—
to be never the one again to act like the rest
but answer to the least of another kind;
to be here no more to savour nor desist,

but to identify maybe the grains of sand
and call anonymous grasses by their name,
to find remembrance if the streets run seabound;
when the tide enters the room, when the roof gives flower
cry Credo to the obdurate weed.

And to have to put up with the pain and process,
nor look back to delight the eyes
that ache with the displacement of all sights.
And to have to alter the trunk of a tree to a dragon
if it should be required, or the river to a swan.

JAN G. ELBURG (1919–1992)

Arcadian Ode

It's turning into milk:
watch how each small sound
and how the light helpful
grows bigger and smaller again while a little sun
dial with hands on it moves on

good is the grass
the meadow is warm with goodly cows
they kneel and pray to the grass
so intently that the flowers turn into cows
so peacefully that the cows offer
their tails a heart of daisies

it's turning into milk, slowly and quietly:
the teats expect the fingers
the shining buckets are waiting
the hairy bumblebees clean
the stalks that are too slender for the wind

Translated from the Dutch by André Lefevere

ROBERT DUNCAN (1919–1988)

TWO POEMS

Often I am Permitted to Return to a Meadow

as if it were a scene made-up by the mind,
that is not mine, but is a made place,

that is mine, it is so near to the heart,
an eternal pasture folded in all thought
so that there is a hall therein

that is a made place, created by light
wherefrom the shadows that are forms fall.

Wherefrom fall all architectures I am
I say are likenesses of the First Beloved
whose flowers are flames lit to the Lady.

She it is Queen Under the Hill
whose hosts are a disturbance of words within words
that is a field folded.

It is only a dream of the grass blowing
east against the source of the sun
in an hour before the sun's going down

whose secret we see in a children's game
of ring a round of roses told.

Often I am permitted to return to a meadow
as if it were a given property of the mind
that certain bounds hold against chaos,

that is a place of first permission,
everlasting omen of what is.

From **The Continent**

There is only the one time.
There is only the one god.
There's only the one promise

and from its flame
the margins of the page flare forth.
There's only the one page,

the rest remains
in ashes. There is only
the one continent, the one sea—

moving in rifts, churning, enjambing,
drifting feature from feature.

ALAIN BOSQUET (1919–1998)

From Of the Material

The sea: the best blood.
The sea: the gesture that unfolds
a sick horizon
and folds again a dawn
like a letter written
to a lost tree.
The sea that slows words down:
their gallop was like that of the waves.
The sea is a peace treaty
between the star and the poem.
The sea, that great height!
The sea, that shell on which
every dreamy octopus rubs itself!
And the seaweed, that algebra!
And the ebb and flow, a theme that becomes drunk
with a word gathered among the coral!
And the island, that mystery of the page
that a sleepwalker carries away like a fruit!
O sea, I am the fable
that you read to me the day you willingly became human!
O sea, you who draft the bibles of silence,
are you now only this drop of water committing suicide?

Translated from the French by Edouard Roditi

LAWRENCE FERLINGHETTI (b. 1919)

From *A Far Rockaway of the Heart*

#33

How the light
      lay on the leaves
How the light
      glinted through them

How the leaves themselves
           were light
How all creatures there
        were light
              were made of light
       the warp of light
            upon them

In the dawn of the world that year

And they
    pulsed with it
          with light of earth
   as if they
        always would be
             full of light
             made of light
Shimmering

Among the sere and yellow leaves

In the autumn of that year

ANONYMOUS (recorded c. 1921)

Two Eskimo Poems

Improvised Song of a Hostess

The lands around my dwelling
Are more beautiful
From the day
When it is given me to see
Faces I have never seen before.
All is more beautiful,
All is more beautiful,
And life is thankfulness.
These guests of mine
Make my house grand.

"I arise from rest"

I arise from rest
With the beat of a raven's wings.
I arise
To meet the day

My eyes turn from the night
To gaze at the dawn
Now whitening.

Translated from the Inuit by Knud Rasmussen

RUARAIDH MACTHÒMAIS (b. 1921)

Sheep

In the still morning the surface of the land was flat,
the wind had died down, its rumbling and thrusting
drowned under its whiteness, each snowflake at rest,
set in its soft fabric like a white blanket.
We had lost the sheep that were out on the moor
when that storm unloaded its burden,
and we spent the morning desperately seeking them.

A storm came over my country,
of fine, deadly, smothering snow:
though it is white, do not believe in its whiteness,
do not set your trust in a shroud;
my heart would rejoice
were I to see on that white plain a yellow spot,
and understand that the breath of the Gael
                        was coming to the surface.

HAYDEN CARRUTH (1921–2008)

Once More

Once more by the brook the alder leaves
turn mauve, bronze, violet, beautiful
after the green of crude summer; galled
black stems, pithy, tangled, twist in the
flesh-colored vines of wild cyclamen.
Mist drifts below the mountaintop
in prismatic tatters. The brook is full,
spilling down heavily, loudly, in silver
spate from the beaver ponds in the high
marshy meadows. The year is sinking:
heavily, loudly, beautifully. Deer move
heavily in the brush like bears, half drunk
on masty acorns and rotten wild apples.
The pileated woodpecker thumps a dead elm
slowly, irregularly, meditatively.
Like a broken telephone a cricket rings
without assertion in dead asters and
goldenrod; asters gone cloudy with seed,
goldenrod burnt and blackened. A gray trout
rests under the lip of glacial stone. One
by one the alder leaves plunge down to earth,
veering, and lie there, glowing, like a shirt
of Nessus. My heart in my ribs does what it
has done occasionally all my life: thumps and
heaves suddenly in irregular rhythm that makes
me gasp. How many times has this season turned
and gone down? How many! I move heavily
into the bracken, and the deer stand still
a moment, uncertain, before they break away,
snorting and bounding heavily before me.

INGER CHRISTENSEN (1921–2008)

Two Poems from *Butterfly Valley: A Requiem*

X
With peace of mind and fragments of sweet lies,
with downy sheen of emerald and jade,
the iris butterfly's bare caterpillars
can camouflage themselves as willow leaves.

I saw them eating their own images
which then were folded into chrysalis
hanging at last like what they simulated,
a leaf among the other clustered leaves.

When with their image-language, butterflies
can use dishonesty and so survive,
then why should I be any less wise,

if it will soothe my terror of the void
to characterize butterflies as souls
and summer visions of the vanished dead.

XI

And summer visions of the vanished dead—
the hawthorn butterfly that hovers like
a white cloud, splashed with deep pink traces
of flowers interwoven by the light;

my grandmother, enfolded in the garden's
thousand fathoms, stock, wallflower, baby's-breath;
my father, who taught me first names of all
the creatures that must creep before they die—

walk with me into the butterfly valley
where everything exists only apart,
where even the dead hear the nightingale.

Its songs glide with an oddly mournful lilt
from lack of suffering to suffering;
my ear gives answer with its deafened ringing.

Translated from the Danish by Susanna Nied

CHAIRIL ANWAR (1922–1949)

Our Garden

Our garden
doesn't spread out very far, it's a little affair
in which we won't lose each other.
For you and me it's enough.
The flowers in our garden don't riot in color.
The grass isn't like a carpet
soft and smooth to walk on.
For us it doesn't matter
because
in our garden
you're the flower, I'm the bee
I'm the bee, you're the flower.
It's small, it's full of sunlight, this garden of ours,
a place where we draw away from the world and from people.

Translated from the Indonesian by Burton Raffel and Nurdin Salam

DENISE LEVERTOV (1923–1997)

A Stone from Iona

Men who planned to be hermits, hoped to be saints, arrived
in a round boat of wicker and skin at a pebbled cove.
Behind them, dangerous leagues of mist and wave
and behind those, a land belov'd and renounced.
    Before them,
beyond the slope of stones and the massed green
spears of iris, waited the island, habitation of birds
and of spirits unknown, dwellers in mounds and hummocks.

Under Columba's saltwashed toes, then jostled beneath
sacks of provisions, and briefly hidden under the coracle
brothers lifted to safety above the tideline, lay
this stone, almost a seabird's egg in form, in color
a white that, placed upon white, is revealed as pearl grey.
Now worn down by fourteen more centuries, its lustre
perhaps has increased, as if moonlight, patiently
blanching and stroking, had aided weather and water
in its perfecting.
                 Hold the stone in your palm:
it fills it, warm when your need is for warmth,
cool when you seek the touch of shadow. Its weight
gives pleasure. One stone is not like another.

BOB KAUFMAN (1925–1986)

Image of Wind

At first extra shadows seemed optical illusions,
Often used to play strange mathematical games.
Self-repeating shadows can be disconcerting to one
Accustomed to creating only one; real madness came
That day shadows began to cast people everywhere.

Only the facelessness of those people, shadow formed,
Made possible the identification most people needed
To prove to themselves that they were themselves, or
At least place themselves among those who counted,
Those who were more than just some shadow's ego, printed.

The fish played games with bows of ships,
As fishermen wove themselves into nets.

Frustrated winds bounced off brick-faced towers,
Whistling over jazzy sobbing in desperate night clubs.

Sometimes, when the wind is blowing in my hair,
I cry, because its coolness is too beautiful.

But usually, I know that rain falls anyway,
Leaving only mud puddles
To catch dead leaves as they fall.
Leaves always fall.
There is nothing to say:
The wind is in charge of lives
Tonight.

EMMETT WILLIAMS (1925–2007)

Synonomy

for Charlotte Moorman and Nam June Paik

the performers are given 26 letters of the alphabet,
    each bearing the figure of an animal.
the performers make sounds consonant (to the performers)
    with each animal-letter they select at random, one by one.
sound sources are determined by the performers.
the animal-letter *a* has the shortest duration, *z* the longest.
the colors of the animal letters determine loudness, but
    which color determines what is left up to the performer

New York
April 1966

ERNESTO CARDENAL (b. 1925)

Stardust

What's in a star? We are.
All the elements of our body and of the planet
were once in the belly of a star.
            We are stardust.
15,000,000,000 years ago we were a mass
of hydrogen floating in space, turning slowly, dancing.
            And the gas condensed more and more
            gaining increasingly more mass
            and mass became star and began to shine.
As they condensed they grew hot and bright.
Gravitation produced thermal energy: light and heat.
That is to say love.
                        Stars were born, grew, and died.
And the galaxy was taking the shape of a flower
the way it looks now on a starry night.
Our flesh and our bones come from other stars
and perhaps even from other galaxies,
we are universal,
and after death we will help to form other stars
and other galaxies.
            We come from the stars, and to them we shall return.

Translated from the Spanish by Jonathan Cohen

PHILIPPE JACCOTTET (b. 1925)

From *Seedtime*

1960
FEBRUARY

"Someone will place in your hand a seed
so that even after your hand's destruction
nothing will have been taken from you or broken."

Words spoken for ignorance of the sequel,
for walking in doubt and in affliction,
confided by folly to the unknown.

Words imprecise, however, or false,
when there can be no question of a gift or a seed
nor of destruction, nor of anything breaking,

When it is a question of defying the grave,
of breaking reason and human semblance
as a prison too narrow and too precise.

Word ventured so as to be more brave
so as to give oneself a bearing more grave
and to clear the air for such a seed.

Translated from the French by Michael Hamburger

ROBERT CREELEY (1926–2005)

From Pictures

for Pen

1
This distance
between pane of glass,
eye's sight—
the far waving green edge

of trees, sun's
reflection, light
yellow—and sky there too
light blue.

2
I will sit here
till breeze, ambient,
enfolds me and I
lift away. I will

sit here as sun
warms my hands, my
body eases, and sounds
grow soft and intimate

in my ears. I will sit
here and the back of the house
behind me will at last
disappear. I will sit here.

9
Wet
        water
warm
        fire.

Rough
        wood
cold
        stone.

Hot
        coals
shining
        star.

Physical hill still my will.
Mind's ambience alters all.

10
As I rode out one morning
just at break of day
a pain came upon me
unexpectedly—

As I thought one day
not to think anymore,
I thought again,
caught, and could not stop—

Were I the horse I rode,
were I the bridge I crossed,
were I a tree
unable to move,

the lake would have
no reflections,
the sweet, soft air
no sounds.

So I hear, I see,
tell still the echoing story
of all that lives in a forest,
all that surrounds me.

CHARLES TOMLINSON (b. 1927)

Harvest

for Paula and Fred

After the hay was baled and stacked in henges,
We walked through the circles in the moonlit field:
The moon was hidden from us by the ranges
Of hills that enclosed the meadows hay had filled.

But its light lay one suffusing undertone
That drew out the day and changed the pace of time:
It slowed to the pulse of our passing feet upon
Gleanings the baler has left on the ground to rhyme

With the colour of the silhouettes that arose,
Dark like the guardians of a frontier strayed across,
Into this in-between of time composed—
Sentries of Avalon, these megaliths of grass.

Yet it was time that brought us to this place,
Time that had ripened the grasses harvested here:
Time will tell us tomorrow that we paced
Last night in a field that is no longer there.

And yet it was. And time, the literalist,
The sense and the scent of it woven in time's changes,
Cannot put by that sweetness, that persistence
After the hay was baled and stacked in henges.

NATHANIEL TARN (b. 1928)

From The Fire Season

c]
Our pines continue to die and continue to die—
funeral carpets of needles around their base.
You could sleep there, you could suffocate
soundly and be in harmony with all of nature.
You no longer know what keeps you from dying,
what keeps you walking, climbing, falling
down to the gullies of a lifelong sleep,
what encouraging music keeps the heart beating:
that surge of live surf in your ears,
the hiss of fire racing through the forest
with a Trojan smile fading among its towers.

d]
We are not far removed from that city. We have
just conquered it. I am not told yet
how many trees it had, how many it has lost.
We were not told to guard its treasures from our fire,
how many centuries of treasure the fire melted down.
There are you see those livid penalties
which strip your face off from your skull,
the lining off your heart and off your muscles,
wearing your knees to bring you down to them.
And you will never swallow them,
never allow the fire to sear your guts,
no, not in a thousand [thousand lifetimes]
because the very life of life for you is justice.

ENRIQUE LIHN (1929–1988)

Swans

    Nearsightedness of swans when they fly,
well rounded and as if brandishing the head,
the neck well stretched.
But even so they don't lose, they gain another
shape of their indisputable beauty
—these luxurious boats of Siegfried,
under whose bulky armor
they made their way to the opera
without losing a single one of their feathers.
    Poetry can rest easy:
it wasn't the swans', it was its own neck
that it wrung in a fit of madness
quite reasonable yet unimportant.
    No mythology or bel canto
can measure up to the ideal swan.

Translated from the Spanish by Jonathan Cohen

GREGORY CORSO (1930–2001)

Stars

Central the hole of creation
Escape hatch from impending light
Uncreatures of space leap out
    Vivid fossils embedded in the night

KAMAU BRAITHWAITE (b. 1930)

From **Yellow Minnim**

for this was the summer the blue-egg
blackeye(d) summ-

ertime.   red combs & proud bronze spurs
now flare themselves in the yards
blue white black brown fluffy & bare-neck hens
scuttle & cluck

in the sea. si-
de sun.   while slowly & tall/ly above them burn
& man-
oeuvre.   the golden galleon clocks

for this is the summer the blue. egg black. eye
summertime

over the fence of the sea. ward yards
comes the sea. weed salt. sea sea. moss
smell

& the flyin fish fly like corn
that is toss thru the drizzling air

sun streaks spread like webs over rock
& the pattern carpets of green purple grass
where a shaggoe crab scuttle. spotted w/coral
& pink

and a starfish closes its eye

the whole wild floor of the bay is like flow-
ing.   like flower-
ing.   flowering.   so that the dark rocks breathe
& the lighted seaweed tremble

the whole wild floor of the bay is like flow-
ing.   like flower-
ing.   flowering.   so that the dark rocks breathe
& the lighted seaweed tremble

& there. cushion & nested bright

in the moss & cracks of the deep green rocks
are the eggs you divinin to fine

& this is the difficult part.   the picking

you have to be still like the line of a kite
or a bee by a flower or a hummingbird mirror
of nature & blurr at the colour of bloom

then carefully cupping the psalm of your hann
so it wdnt be prick by the prick-
les.   you press on the sea egg & pull

it

lifting the white blue little hedgehog head
from the rock like a cup that is stuck
to a saucer

but hole it! doan mine if it tickle the palm
a yu hann.   all the prickles are livin

but hole it! doan mine if it tickle the psalm
a you hann & down back down for another

in the end you shd have from two to tree
pairs cradle into the crook a yu harvess.   each
pair like the firss one.   face-touchin-face

yu is ress for a minit.   holdin on to de world
a de wood a de rock-

in boat & yu breathe

in.   *one two tree,*   an then
down is back
dung under the water

all the sky blue air you cd hole in you chess
in you chess & de ress store up in yu belly
eyes wide.   eyes red.   body curve/in down to de

spine down down along de spine to hole
de air better & give yu-self
time

so is dung back dung for annudda

rock bruise prick. le
finger.   rippin & robin & rapin
the ripenin blue egg black. eye summertime sea-

son

GARY SNYDER (b. 1930)

Running Water Music

under the trees
under the clouds
by the river
on the beach,

"sea roads."
whales   great sea-path beasts—

              salt;   cold
              water;   smoky fire.
steam, cereal,
              stone, wood boards.
bone awl, pelts,
              bamboo pins and spoons.
unglazed bowl.
a band around the hair.

              beyond wounds.

sat on a rock in the sun,
watched the old pine
wave
over blinding fine white
              river sand.

HANS FAVEREY (1930–1990)

"Spring it must be"

Spring, it must be. Persephone,

a little absent-mindedly still, opens
her satin peignoir, folds her hands
behind her head, breathes in deeply, holds

her breath a moment, and breathes out deeply,
deeply. Now, accustomed to the light,
she starts to see what she knew,
hardly perturbed by what she

knows must come. Her eyes are hazel,

her hair ashblonde, but her neck
has the scent of now and never.
Oh, kidlike it bounded forward,
and licked the milk from her shell.

Translated from the Dutch by Francis R. Jones

JEROME ROTHENBERG (b. 1931)

The Nature Theatre of Oklahoma (6)

"you are a bear" she said
& he became
a bear, he wore it
like his skin
the lost look
the interior grace
that surfaced on him,
he was faceless too
& walked inside
his footsteps   half
an animal who loves
his other half,
the silence of the moon
over his head,
this is the mark the man's arm
scribbles, darkly,
on the cave wall,
in the cave,
in oklahoma

KAZUKO SHIRAISHI (b. 1931)

Summer Time—The Full Moon Four Days After July 27th

my mother silently went to heaven   four days ago
and tonight   is the full moon
my mother quietly completed her work
                        the last penance called living
when she breathed in and exhaled   as if reaching
as far back as to the Inca Empire
                        the thin river of her life
                                trembled like a thread

now everything is fine
she is   happier than the moon   she does not have to
        wander about
                        among the dark clouds

she does not have to   shine serenely
                and slowly leave
she has obtained   the permanence
of her existence by not existing   ah
I forgot to say, thank you   because your leaving
this world was   too soon   and too quiet a sigh

what is called permanence is   transient
because it only exists inside me
in this finite inside
infinity   that is a permanence is   now
                                floating

ah   full moon
              please shine
on my beloved   my mother
          please flutter
        like a spring breeze
      quietly over the repose of her soul
          like
                drops of light

Translated from the Japanese by Yumiko Tsumura and Samuel Grolmes

TOMAS TRANSTRÖMER (b. 1931)

The Blue Wind-Flowers

To be spellbound—nothing's easier. It's one of the oldest tricks of the soil and springtime: the blue wind-flowers. They are in a way unexpected. They shoot up out of the brown rustle of last year in overlooked places where one's gaze never pauses. They glimmer and float—yes, float—from their color. The sharp violet-blue now weighs nothing. Here is ecstasy, but low voiced. "Career"—irrelevant! "Power" and "publicity"—ridiculous! They must have given a great reception up in Nineveh, with pompe and "Trompe up!" Raising the rafters. And above all those brows the crowning crystal chandeliers hung like glass vultures. Instead of such an over-decorated and strident cul-de-sac, the wind-flowers open a secret passage to the real celebration, quiet as death.

Translated from the Swedish by Robin Fulton

DAVID ANTIN (b. 1932)

From The River

      san diego is like the end of the united states and
its really very beautiful in a strange way   but it was
beautiful before they got here from kansas and oklahoma
    part of it they neglected and that has remained
beautiful   but what they didnt neglect hasnt remained
beautiful   because they decided that san diego was on the
    mediterranean   they had a strange sense of geography
      they decided they had landed on the algerian coast   so
    they put up palm trees date palms   but they also imported
      korean grass and bougainvillea and australian sweet gum
    trees   and after a generation of feeding these exotic
    blooms with water from the north they began to think of them
as native flora   and the australian eucalyptus flourished

      they had imported it in the 1880s to provide ties
for the railroad   and its wood was not good enough   but
southern california is a lot like the australian desert
    so the eucalyptus flourished anyway   and the farmers
    thought to use rows of eucalyptus as windbreaks for their
mediterranean orange trees   which didnt flourish without
    the provision of lots and lots of water   because san diego
is very much like the australian desert   in which it rains
    rarely and heavily   that is when it rains it often rains
heavily but it is a rare occasion
                        from june to october it
    almost never rains   hardly a drop of rain   there is sun
and sun and more son except for an overcast morning or
    evening   and there isnt a drop of rain for months on end
    this untroubled place dries and dries and dries   yet
trees flourish   luxuriant palms and jacaranda and orange
    trees and olives   green tentacles extend all over san
diego   supported by water coming down from the north or
    from the east   which they send down to grow these strange
    things that they exhibit to tourists as the native thing

because now nearly nobody remembers what native forms there
were   except in a few places spotted irregularly around the
   county
              we live on a patch of native growth   three acres of
chaparral   you let it alone and it grows   we live on
   three acres of it it keeps people away because its like a
   thicket and its marvelously fragrant and hospitable for
birds coyotes and small deer and we like it   but we're on
   the outside   and being on the outside is like being at the
beginning

ALAN GROSSMAN (b. 1932)

From Poland of Death (V)

There are many waves when there is wind at sea.
Each wave has a history which ends, it seems, at the shore.
Or it begins again, there, in another form—in thunder,
Or in a proverb, or with a sigh. On the shore are
Often many stones. What then? *What then?* Each one is
Perfect, and each is a cause of dissatisfaction to me.
Each one is whole and each is a fragment of a greater whole,
Finite or infinite stones: minds, or glimpses of mind.
Which one is the stone of witness? For one is the stone
Of witness. It may or may not be on this shore, or on
The countless shores everywhere. But where it is it hears
The proverb of the waters on windy nights in Summer,
And at noon in Autumn watery sighs, and on Winter mornings
The thunder of the wave when there is wind at sea.
In Spring the stone of witness sees the wave fall down
Upon the shore. And then rise from its fall, shaken,
In another form, and climb to the shore road which it
Crosses—to hear the blackbirds sing in the marshland.

MICHAEL McCLURE (b. 1932)

A Spirit of Mount Tamalpais

	DEER BONES AND FOX SCATS
	dry in the late
	spring sun
	watched over
	by
	yellow mule-ears
	and blue-eyed grass.
Buckwheat	Cries
Brodiaea	of hummingbirds
Bunch grass	in
A vulture (close)	the
Bee plant	wind
Crab spider	on
Garter snake	the path
Seaside daisy	through
Grindelia	the chaparral.
Coyote bush	Bright
Poison oak	vision
Cow parsnip	light.
Wild iris	Ocean
Baeria	below.
Buttercup	Hello,
	Lew!

GENNADY AYGI (1934–2007)

Two Poems

Clouds

it was
as if
in God was the head
but remaining alone then
and it became clear: Day was darkening (there was work
    to be done)
and was shining – as it opened!
what was happening was consciousness – no doubt
it was melting with smallness-me
in That – which was opening the clouds like gates
forcing the mind – to shine! – and the frontiers
were time: were the breaks
in the vividly-single
(touching the Earth)

White Butterfly Flying over a Cut Field

Translated from the Russian by Peter France

GUSTAF SOBIN (1935–2005)

Fragment: From a Blossoming Almond

for Theo

where bees
shadow-
box with the wind-
shuttled buds,
the

image de-
taches, gets

sent . . . .
. . . .
. . . . wrought
tokens, our
breath-

studded screens . . .
shall
sleep in the lee of
that

tremor, move
to
the cold

shaken scale of its
petals.

From **At the Sea**

Down to the shore. And smell of brine. Away from moss, fern, mortar, brick. Form is fatal, some say. Whereas an endless unborn surface. Without point. Of reference. Containment. Or even vanishing.

*

Here where the light is. Less hidden? Less dispersed into less things? Rolls in. White-crested. Splendor after splendor. Wall piled on wall. High as a house. And down comes crashing. Rocks. Severed heads. Centuries. And from the sand a thin veil of white recedes. And ripples and shadows and a ledge of clouds lined orange.

*

Seeing is believing. But unthreatened by the dark are words. And there take refuge. Unshadowed. And thinking too takes refuge and then its own seed of light tries to sow.

*

Pounding pounding the waves. Breath skyward drawn. Out of observable space, of muscular intuition. And the light goes on pretending that seeing is simple. That with mine own eyes have I touched. The shell in the sand. The fin of the minnow.

*

I know the creed of light. We see. On condition of not seeing. The light. Transparent we dream the immediate.

SUSAN HOWE (b. 1937)

From *Cabbage Gardens*

Worn out man
knocking at his father's door

am alone aloud

and my throat turns

saying

beauty of winter about Her

hair as dark
as the trees in the forest

against white snow.

Place of importance as in the old days
stood on the ramparts of the fort
                                        the open sea outside
alone with water-birds and cattle
                        knee-deep in a stream
grove of reeds
                herons watching from the bank
henges
        whole fields honeycombed with souterrains
human
                        bones through the gloom
        whose sudden mouth
surrounded my face
                        a thread of blue around the coast
                                        feathery moon
eternity swallows up time
                                peaceable as foam
                O cabbage gardens
summer's elegy
                sunset survived

JOSÉ EMILIO PACHECO (b. 1939)

The Octopus

Dark god of the depths,
fern, toadstool, hyacinth,
between the unseen rocks, through the abyss there
in the dawn, against the currents of strong sunlight
night sinks to the sea floor, and from the cups of its tentacles
the octopus sips in black ink. So sweet and crystalline
that most penumbral brine of mother water
is to that midnight beauty, if it goes
tacking to and fro. But on the beach, littered
with plastic trash, this carnal jewel of viscous vertigo
trails like a long-limbed gorgon; and now with sticks
/ they're battering / that stranded udder.
Someone has hurled a harpoon, and the octopus sucks in death
through this fresh suffocation that constitutes its wound.
No blood wells from its lips; night bursts—
pitching the sea into mourning.
And through it slowly, sadly, as the octopus expires
the earth vanishes.

Translated from the Spanish by George McWhirter

HOMERO ARIDJIS (b. 1940)

Hangzhou

for Jan Hendrix

Mist-covered lake.
Lost image of the day's
untold story;
unseeing eye of water, where
the sun lays the tracks of forgetting.
White glow of the mind,
of a crane or a god.
The tree, a fixed passenger
in the eternity of the moment.
She and I look through the window
at clouds forming
intangible bestiaries.
Everything is moving toward its end.
Everything appears to be standing still,
but going, too. Including me.
Only a phantasmal bird
crosses the threshold of the eye.

Translated from the Spanish by George McWhirter

W. G. SEBALD (1944–2001)

TWO POEMS

Like a dog

Cézanne says
that's how a painter
must see, the eye
fixed & almost
averted

*

Blue

grass
seen
through a thin
layer
of frozen
water

Translated from the German by Michael Hamburger

MICHAEL PALMER (b. 1943)

Two Poems

Finisterrae

The eye on each wing, for example,
many have mentioned this.

That it sees nothing,
no one has mentioned this.

Anode (27 VIII 96–26 V 99)

What shadow lights
the buddings of salt

spiral of rock
syntax of rust

grammar of bone
fistfuls of dust

(to the travelers—L. M., N. C.)

BERNADETTE MAYER (b. 1945)

Wren Warbler Sonnet

the wind is blowing on one of those
innocent days, this year we became
landlords of birds on the front porch
robins, starlings, wrens, warblers
they pay no rent, we clean up their shit
once in the warbler nest there was a squabble
feathers & nest stuff everywhere, i had seen
a wren go into the warbler enclave, maybe
i was mistaken, perhaps for a visit
just one bird to another, on my plate i put
all the downed feathers covered by petrified rock
i thought, i am way too involved with these birds
    next day a warbler said to me
    that wren is a terrorist, report him

From Song of the Andoumboulou: 58

      Scrounged around on what earth was
left, the intransigent few Nub stubbed
    its toe on. All of earth was what
earth was left so few we were, back
                            at

    some beginning it seemed. . . It was
      morning, gray morning, pearl divers
    chanting in the Gulf beside the
bed, clock dial phosphorescent, lit.
      The lovers lay again without
                      recoil,
      world without war without end
        intimated, dream they'd awaken
   from. . . In a ship's hold helpless,
                 hair
    the look of thicket, ship of state they'd
                     call
    it, crushed. . . But for now, before that,
  sleep of ages, again as if starting
from scratch. Asleep yet on the tips of
                 their
    tongues kept asking, salt not known to
                  call itself
  salty, what to
say

.

WILL ALEXANDER (b. 1948)

From The Sri Lankan Loxodrome

you see
by collecting psychic data
from the Sri Lankan Central Hills
I've been equated to the role of an intermittent vampire
to a blue convulsive shark
deaf with irregular nesting
my body being listed
as a hunchbacked "squid"
as a ravenous mahimahi
equated to birds beneath the sea

& the sound of melted coastal ice
parallel with living my life
in a sightless hurricane cellar
trenchantly kept alive
by old biography or germs
yet obsessed by the abyss
being verdurous & inward with scintillation

I know the Omosudis lowei
the yellow-greenish "Globigerina"
the various shark fish which glow inside their absence
so I am ancient
without body

BEI DAO (b. 1949)

Sleep, Valley

Sleep, valley
with blue mist quickly cover the sky
and the wild lilies' pale eyes
Sleep, valley
with rainsteps quickly chase away the wind
and the anxious cries of the cuckoo

Sleep, valley
here we hide
as if in a thousand-year dream
time no longer glides past blades of grass
stopped behind layers of clouds, the sun's clock
no longer swings down evening glow or dawn

Spinning trees
toss down countless hard pine cones
protecting two lines of footprints
our childhoods walked with the seasons
along this winding path
and pollen drenched the brambles

Ah, it's so quiet and still
the cast stone has no echo
perhaps you are searching for something
—from heart to heart
a rainbow rises in silence
—from eye to eye

Sleep, valley
sleep, wind
valley, asleep in blue mist
wind, asleep in our hands

Translated from the Chinese by Bonnie McDougall

ELIOT WEINBERGER (b. 1949)

From Dreams from the Holothurians

Atlantis! In the dark the holothurians eat and excrete and move on and eat, inching forward, thinking, sending out their mental flares in the hope that someone, something, anything will drop by and relieve the tedium of their biological fate, down there, at the bottom of the sea, with the calcified sponges, magnesium nodules, the crushed spines of sea urchins, the ghosts of coelenterates, unexploded torpedoes, skeletons of bathypterids and halosaurs, the hieroglyphic tracks of sea pens and ophiuroids, fecal coils, the waving arms of a burrowed brittle-star, manganese-encrusted dolphin teeth, the remains of a jettisoned crate of manilla-envelope clasps, zeolite crystals, pillows of basalt, calcareous shells of pteropods, the sinister egg-casings of skates, the broken anti-matter locks from a crashed spaceship, the short-crested ripples of sand, and the scour moats forming in globigerina ooze.

ANNE CARSON (b. 1950)

God's Justice

In the beginning there were days set aside for various tasks.
On the day He was to create justice
God got involved in making a dragonfly

and lost track of time.
It was about two inches long
with turquoise dots all down its back like Lauren Bacall.

God watched it bend its tiny wire elbows
as it set about cleaning the transparent case of its head.
The eye globes mounted on the case

rotated this way and that
as it polished every angle.
Inside the case

which was glassy black like the windows of a downtown bank
God could see the machinery humming
and He watched the hum

travel all the way down turquoise dots to the end of the tail
and breathe off as light.
Its black wings vibrated in and out.

TAKASHI HIRAIDE (b. 1950)

Two Poems from *For the Fighting Spirit of the Walnut*

57
Spirits wrapped in a skin of green. On each one, lushly growing,
a hanging drop of thunderstorm!

83
One day, in the afternoon after the rain, on the escalator going
from the west side of the first floor to the second floor of the
Takashimaya store in Nihonbashi, I saw a single snail in front of
me, and found myself sighing deeply at the pointlessness of his
rhyme. Would he now proceed to the greenery on the rooftop,
or head straight to the kitchen of the main dining hall. Or per-
haps he has some shopping to do. At least get yourself up to the
magic section, little spiral. I whispered words of encouragement,
but all I saw was maybe a shy little twitch of the tentacles.

Translated from the Japanese by Sawako Nakayasu

CORAL BRACHO (b. 1951)

Two Poems

Butterfly

Like a spinning coin
threaded to the sun
the butterfly catching fire
at the sweet basil flower.

Water's Lubricious Edges

Water of jellyfish,
lacteal, sinuous water,
water of lubricious borders; glassy thinkness—Deliquesence
in delectable contours. Water—sumptuous water
of involution, of languor

in placid densities. Water,
water silken and plumbeous in opacity, in weight—Mercurial;
    water in suspense, slow water. The algal bloom
brilliant—In the paps of pleasure. The algae, the
    bracing vapor of its peak;

—across the arched silence, across isthmuses
of basalt; the algae, its habitual rub,
its slippage. Light water, fish water; the aura, the agate,
its luminous border-breakings; Fire trailing the fleeing

elk—Around the ceiba tree, around the shoal of fish; flame
pulsing;
lynx water, sargo water (The sudden jasper). Luminescence
of jellyfish.
—Edge open, lipped; aura of lubricious borders,
its smoothness rocking, its nesting efflorescence; amphibious,
labile—Water, water silken
with voltaic charge; expectant. Water in suspense, slow water—
    The lascivious luminescence

in its oily crossing,
over faulted basalt. —The slither of opal through the sheen,
through the interior flame. —Water
of jellyfish.
Soft, lustrous water;
traceless water; dense,
mercurial
    its steely whiteness, its dissolution in graphite surges,
in burnished gloss; furtive, smooth. —Living water

upwelling ventral over dorsal, capsized bronze sun enfolding
—crystalline zinc, spouting water. Water of jellyfish, tactile water
fusing itself
to the unctuous indigo blue, to its reverberant honeycomb.
    Amianthus, ulva water
The catfish in its silt
—sucking; in the nutritious essence, in its delicate nectar; the
    aureous
reservoir, a limbo, transparentizes it. Light water, aura within amber
—graceful, anointed luminance; the tiger, its high tide
below the brittle shadow. Boundary water, eel water licking
    its profile,
its nocturnal migration
—In silk matrices; in the sage. —Water

between the hake. Gravid water (—The calm pleasure
tepid; its iridescence) —Water
its borders

—Its shifting smoothness, its enchantment
with what is nubile,
cadenced. Water,
silky water of involution, of languor
in placid densities. Water, water;   Its caress
—Otter water, fish water. Water

of jellyfish,
lacteal, sinuous water; Water,

Translated from the Spanish by Forrest Gander

164

JIMMY SANTIAGO BACA (b. 1952)

From *Meditations on the South Valley*

XII
I am remembering the South Valley.
Rain smacked tin-roofs
like an all night passenger train,
fiery flames of moon flashing
from the smoke stack.
Beneath the rain shaded sky,
faint surge of rain pulsing down my windows,
rain's blue mouth curling around everything,
                            I dream
myself maiz root
swollen in pregnant earth,
rain seeping into my black bones
sifting red soil grains of my heart
into earth's hungry mouth.

I am part of the earth.

ROBERTO BOLAÑO (1953–2003)

Rain

It's raining and you say *it's as if the clouds*
were crying. Then cover your mouth and speed up
your step. As if those emaciated clouds were crying?
Impossible. So then, why all this rage,
This desperation that'll bring us all to hell?
Nature hides some of her methods
in Mystery, her stepbrother. And so, sooner than
you think, this afternoon you consider
an afternoon of the apocalypse, will seem nothing but
a melancholy afternoon, an afternoon of loneliness lost
in memory: Nature's mirror. Or maybe
you'll forget it. Rain, weeping, your footsteps
resounding on the cliff-walk. They don't matter.
Right now you can cry and let your image dissolve
on the windshields of cars parked along
the Boardwalk. But you can't lose yourself.

Translated from the Spanish by Laura Healy

GU CHENG (1956–1993)

From **Eulogy to the World**

7. *Inside the Bottle*
Through the tiny glass mouth
of the life in which we reside
we can see the world above

Crows plunge straight into the sea
we can see roses and the seedy heads of cattails

We'll never reach the roses
nor touch the soft green threads of earth

22. *After the Air Raid Had Passed*
After the air raid had passed
we began to speak of poetry again
the ground soaking wet
everywhere lay shattered pottery

Just then you walked in
carrying a basket weighty
with food that you brought for me
bread and golden honey

Just two weeks after your death
I too died there in battle
emerald green grasses
now sealing up this trench

37. *Nature*

I'm fond of that once-thrown spear
the ten thousand leaves in the tree
military troops crowding the earth

They show just their faces along the long, narrow road
ponderously waving their bird-nest banners
This is the subtle place where life fails

47. *Afternoon's Silver Bracelet*

It won't be over even if this money is all spent
and we need not be worried and conceal our age
never understanding anything about this world
we treasure its fog and mists
our hats plucked off by gusts of wind

Beasts stand elegantly by the wall
we cannot pick up our hats with our toes

Translated from the Chinese by Joseph R. Allen

FORREST GANDER (b. 1956)

Terror

Before the pulse of severe cold, in sand
beneath the arborescent heather's
                              bleak twigs,
a bluebottle fly lays its eggs in the slit of a dead starling's beak.

Who is inaccessible to fear? Startle reflex:
                              that revulsion
prior to the moment of being, a spasm
before self comes to life and fills in
the interval with a perception called pain, charging
                              the body with nausea.
A civil war in my face? Is this hunger unlike that of others?
I look up toward the earth's gleaming, silverdark rim:
the lour of cumulus, relinquished
kindness, dusk's faltering measure. And down.

Was it insignificant before I bent
my gorgeous attention over it?

PETER COLE (b. 1957)

From Why Does the World Out There Seem

1.
Why does the natural feel unnatural?
Why does the world out there seem
so utterly foreign to these poems?
It isn't strange, and hardly hostile,
to the heart and eye behind their lines:
dirt exploding into spring,
leaves climbing the pipe to the screen,
the morning glory's funnel of blue,
the sap of it all coursing through
every fiber of all those veins.
Why does the natural feel so strained
when set beside the abstract figures
of speech's discourse linking us?
Poems, as Williams wrote, are machines.

5.
Amusement derives from the animal's mouth
and snout, stuck there in the air,
as it stares, struck by words
it heard. In a manner of speaking
it muzzles as in what's not fair,
or wonder. And in the illogical moment
of what it means and how it works,
while the mouth is closed, nourishment—
if it's serious—enters through it.
And in a nutshell that's the sentence
and solace that sweet Chaucer meant.
The poem's gesture, changing, survives
in generations of aspiration,
leading us on . . . or into our lives.

DUNYA MIKHAIL (b. 1965)

From *Diary of a Wave Outside the Sea*

We made room in our day for every star,
and our dead remained without graves.

We wrote the names of each flower on the walls
and we, the sheep, drew the grass
—our favorite meal—
and we stood with our arms open to the air
so we looked like trees.
All this to change the fences into gardens.
A naïve bee was tricked and smashed into a wall,
flying toward what it thought was a flower.
Shouldn't the bee be able to fly over the fence-tops?

Long lines are in front of us.
Standing, we count flasks of flour on our fingers
and divide the sun among the communicating vessels.

We sleep standing in line
and the experts think up plans for vertical tombs
because we will die standing.

We are scenery lacking everything;
existing, if not for the existence of politics.

Our flowers scale the walls in dreams.

Widows dream of storks
dropping the missing down the chimney.

And orphans enter the underground tunnels
believing they are long kisses.

Every day we praise God
and we endure the spit of the devil,
then we pray for the sake of the homeland,
our lost paradise.
Every day, they fill jars with words or wars;
every day we shatter the jars.

The war merchants sell the air
and glorify medals made of tin;
and girls comb the wheat each day
and sift the clouds into bowls
so that cotton rises over their heads
just like the revolutions that rise
in a white dress, and the girls
don't know if it is a shroud
or a wedding dress!

Translated from the Arabic by Elizabeth Winslow

THALIA FIELD (b. 1966)

From Parting

/Earth layers/
core, mantle, crust. We think of pit, flesh, and skin
of fruit; a fruit's sweet near-nothing mixed with
the impulse to consume the life layer, so thin it
practially wipes off.

. . .

/Sand/
quartz, sandstone, or feldspar polished in the swash action of
waves. Silt and clay sands are shale. Clay particles are finest,
red with iron, black with decayed organic matter. Along eroded
cliffs, large streaks of garnet, while tropical sand shines white
with broken shell fragments and corals, calcite minerals and
the excrement of crustaceans, echinoderms. Acidic water added
back converts sand to limestone; now loose, now land-maker.

. . .

/Plankton/
all the drifting life of the ocean.

LULJETA LLESHANAKU (b. 1968)

Frost

Predictably, the first frost arrived
simplifying what we saw.
The atmosphere began to hibernate
into the realm of hypothesis.

First you touched the inviting flora of my eyes
then the untrodden earth
with its subtle memory of grain
(my fingers now held tight).
Then, after the clay, you touched upon
our ancient apprehensions, irresponsibility,
vengeance for a story left untold.

And on and on until you reached a layer of water.
Can you hear it flowing?
This is my vivid core, you can't go any deeper.
And yet you do . . . further and further. We were wrong.
Here the elemental world of cold metals begins—
here identity, weight, gravitational forces end,
where I can no longer be I.

Frost arrived, the scene sufficiently simplified
the sound of an accordion, roads cordoned off,
breath freezing at the first syllable
turning to beautiful coral
transforming into coral.

Translated from the Albanian by Henry Israeli and Shpresa Qatipi

Envoy: Passages 7

Good Night,   at last
the light of the sun is gone
under the Earth's rim
and we
can see the dark   interstices
Day's lord erases.

—Robert Duncan

Index of Poets & Translators

(Translators are in italic. An asterisk signifies both poet and translator.)

177

Index of Titles

Sources & Acknowledgments

All of the poems in this anthology were previously published in New Directions editions. The year of publication is noted in parenthesis after each New Directions title. The entries appear below in order of appearance in the book (unless poems by different poets were pulled from the same volume, in which case these were consolidated into one entry). Thanks to all the authors, translators, agents, executors, and estates for their kind permission to reprint these poems and translations.

Anonymous, *The Book of Odes* from *The Confucian Odes: The Classic Anthology Defined by Confucius* by Ezra Pound (1959). Published by Harvard University Press as *Shih-Ching: The Classical Anthology Defined by Confucius.* Translation copyright © 1954, 1982 by the President and Fellows of Harvard College.

Sappho, "Come out of Crete" and Herakleitos, "The Logos is eternal" from *7 Greeks* by Guy Davenport (1995). Translation copyright © 1995 by Guy Davenport.

Euripides, *Hippolytus Temporizes & Ion* by H.D. (2003). Copyright © 1927, 1937 by Hilda Aldington. Translation copyright © 1986, 2003 by The Schaffner Family Foundation.

Euripides, *Medea* and Robinson Jeffers, *Cawdor* from *Cawdor and Medea* by Robinson Jeffers (1970). Translation copyright © 1928, 1946, 1956 by Robinson Jeffers. Copyright © 1970 by Donnan Call Jeffers & Garth Sherwood Jeffers.

Prince Ilangô Adigal, "The Blessings" from *Shilappadikaram (The Ankle Bracelet)* (1965). Translation copyright © 1965 by Alain Daniélou.

Meleagros, "Flowers: For Hêliodôra" from *Poems from the Greek Anthology* by Dudley Fitts (1956). Translation copyright © 1938, 1941, 1956 by New Directions.

Lucretius, "Darling of Gods and Men"; Manuchehri, "The thundercloud fills meadows"; Sa'di, "Night swallowed the sun" from *Basil Bunting: Complete Poems* (2000). Translation copyright © 2000 by the Estate of Basil Bunting.

Virgil, *Georgics: I* from *Spring Shade: Poems 1931–1970* by Robert Fitzgerald (1971). Translation copyright © 1971 by Robert Fitzgerald.

King Shudraka, "The Toy Cart" from *Great Sanskrit Plays*, edited by P. Lal (1964). Translation copyright © 1964 by P. Lal.

Ovid, *Amores* [Book I, Elegy 13], translated by Christopher Marlowe; Geoffrey Chaucer, "Roundel" from *Parlement of Foules*; Christopher Marlowe, "I walked along a stream"; William Shakespeare, Song from *As You Like It* [Act II, Scene 7]; and Christopher Smart, *Jubilate Agno* from *Confucius to Cummings: An Anthology of Poetry*, edited by Ezra Pound and Marcella Span (1964).

T'ao Ch'ien, "Turning Seasons" from *Mountain Home: The Wilderness Poetry of Ancient China*, edited and translated by David Hinton (2005). Translation copyright © 2002, 2005 by David Hinton.

Hsieh Ling-Yün, "Dwelling in the Mountains" from *The Mountain Poems of Hsieh Ling-Yün* (2001). Translation copyright © 2001 by David Hinton.